BLINDSIDED

BY

The Coming Paradigm Shift

A New Look

"The wise shall understand"
Daniel 12:10

B.T. Moore

Blindsided by the Coming Paradigm Shift

Published by B.T. Moore, P.O. Box 783, Sulphur, Oklahoma 73086

Unless otherwise noted, all Scripture quotations are from the King James Version of the Bible.

Scripture quotations marked NLT are from the Holy Bible, New Living Translation ©.

Scripture quotations marked ESV are from the Holy Bible, English Standard Version ©.

Note: All fully capitalized words, underlining, and parenthesis used in scripture quotations are (MY OWN) **EMPHASIS**

ISBN 978-0-578-04884-0

Evangelist B.T. Moore has traveled extensively preaching and teaching in thirty-three states and three foreign countries bringing gospel messages to churches, retreat gatherings, camps, and conferences.

His emphasis for the past five years has been upon the messages of Revelation for today's church. Using Power Point slides and other visual aids, he has brought renewed interest to a topic that has so long seemed confusing and complex to so many earnest Christians.

Evangelist Moore is the founder of Loving Hands Ranch in Oklahoma, a Camping program for Deaf youth. See website: **www.lovinghandsranch.com**

You can contact him at the following addresses:

B.T. Moore
P.O. Box 783
Sulphur, OK 73086

Email: **btm2@brightok.net**

TABLE OF CONTENTS

Blindsided

Who has not seen a football player blindsided on the field of play? He's running down the field fully aware of the path he has in mind, totally focused on his objective, completely absorbed by his destination; when suddenly, without any perception of an approaching opponent, he is caught totally unprepared to deal with the massive, shocking, sometimes, harmful collision with another player who is also totally focused, but focused on rendering him irrelevant to the development of the play. We automatically cringe when we see the defenseless player absolutely devastated by the blow. We practically feel his pain as he crumples to the ground in a heap of pain and bewilderment. Many times the player is not only shocked and hurt by the blow from the opponent but also by the weird and unprotected way he hits the ground. Sometimes he is carried or helped off the field where everyone hopes he'll recover.

This hurtful and vulnerable scenario will one day be played out on a much grander field of play, and in much more painful reality for the Church of the Lord Jesus Christ. Ironically, the approaching calamity is not our destiny, but our choice by negligence. Few Christians are aware of our Savior's repeated warnings about the approaching impact and its consequent pain and devastation. And, fewer yet are aware of his instructions on how to avoid the coming cosmic collision. Let me share a few quotes from our concerned Lord and Savior, Jesus Christ. Here's one that he addressed to some of his closest disciples:

And take heed to yourselves, lest at any time your hearts be overcharged with surfeiting, and drunkenness, and cares of this life, and so that day come upon you unawares. For as a snare shall it come on all them that dwell on the face of the whole earth. Watch ye therefore, and pray always, that ye may be accounted worthy to escape all these things that shall come to pass, and to stand before the Son of man. Luke 21:34-36

Hmmm... seems like the Master viewed some as being counted

1

worthy to escape a very terrible event or set of events coming upon every person living on the planet. Something of terrible consequence is going to be unleashed on this earth in the same manner that a trap is suddenly sprung on its unsuspecting victim. Jesus is addressing his own people and warning them about this upcoming world-wide tragedy. Surely, you might think, Jesus would never allow an awful thing like that to happen to his own church! One thing we can say for sure about this passage, "Jesus doesn't want his own servants to be blindsided at the time of it's release". Another most interesting thing becomes obvious by our Savior's warning: If being a born-again Christian was enough to avoid this impending world-wide disaster, then Jesus would not have bothered warning his disciples about the possibility of their own lives falling into peril. And so a portrait of the church's future begins to take form with a striking call to avoid being blindsided by a cataclysmic, world-wide horror destined to affect every living person on the planet at the time of its release.

Perhaps you are still reticent to accept the possibility of Christians (members of Jesus own body) being affected by such a traumatic world-encompassing holocaust. If so, then it might be wise to understand what Jesus was conveying in <u>Revelation 3:14-16</u>

And unto the angel of the church of the Laodiceans write; These things saith the Amen, the faithful and true witness, the beginning of the creation of God; I know thy works, that thou art neither cold nor hot: I would thou wert cold or hot. So then because thou art lukewarm, and neither cold nor hot, I will spue thee out of my mouth.

Many things can be said about this verse that are vitally important to the church. One thing definitely stands out in vivid clarity; Jesus has declared that there are those of His own church who are going to be spewed out of His mouth as if they were repugnant and unpalatable. Not surprisingly, this is spoken to the last church addressed by our Savior in the Book of Revelation. Many Bible scholars agree that this seventh church encompasses in a special way, the final era of the church age which began with Jesus and His apostles, and concludes with the return of our Savior from heaven.

If so, then those who will be "spewed out of his mouth" are among those who are present in the earth at the close of the Church age. This makes the spitting out of Christians even more vital to our own understanding. We must know what Jesus meant by this repulsive illustration of some in his own Church. Little wonder that Jesus repeated seven times in Revelation Chapters 2 and 3... *"He that hath an ear, let him hear what the Spirit saith unto the churches"*. The responsibility is obviously our own to learn what Jesus is saying to us in our present time.

Another passage in the Bible casts even more light on the subject we are currently assessing i.e. the impending collision of some members of the church with a furious episode of horror, pain, and conflict at the end of the age. It is found in Matthew chapter 25. One of the things that makes chapter 25 so interesting and connected with the subject we are contemplating, is the timing and placement of the words spoken by Jesus in this chapter. Those who are familiar with the Gospel of Matthew chapter 24 know that Jesus gives an account of end time events leading up to His return to earth. His own disciples requested to know when Jesus would come; and when he would establish His Kingdom and do away with the kingdoms of this world. For them, "the end" was of vital interest. Jesus listed a comprehensive list of various events and warnings that would lead up to the moment of His return in Chapter 24. Remarkably, Jesus begins Chapter 25 this way:

Then shall the kingdom of heaven be likened unto ten virgins, which took their lamps, and went forth to meet the bridegroom.

In this chapter, Jesus sets forth a parable that describes how things will be in the Kingdom of heaven or in the Church if you will. This is not a parable about the world, or Satan's Kingdom, or unbelievers. It is a descriptive parable of the way things will be for the saints at the end of the age that Jesus had just set forth in Chapter 24. Most of us are quite familiar with the parable and have heard it over and over. Ten virgins are involved in a reception of the Groom who will come and get his bride. Their job is to carry the lamps that light the way for the groom when he comes for his bride.

Interestingly, Jesus sums up only two categories of Christians at the time leading up to his coming. One category includes the "wise" and the other encompasses the "foolish". There is no other category mentioned or available for the saints at this time. Saints are simply, wise or foolish in the eyes of our savior at this time. Now notice what the parable indicates about the circumstances of these two classes of Saints.

And five of them were wise, and five were foolish. They that were foolish took their lamps, and took no oil with them: But the wise took oil in their vessels with their lamps. While the bridegroom tarried, they all slumbered and slept. And at midnight there was a cry made, Behold, the bridegroom cometh; go ye out to meet him. Then all those virgins arose, and trimmed their lamps. And the foolish said unto the wise, Give us of your oil; for our lamps are gone out. But the wise answered, saying, Not so; lest there be not enough for us and you: but go ye rather to them that sell, and buy for yourselves. And while they went to buy, the bridegroom came; and they that were ready went in with him to the marriage: and the door was shut. Afterward came also the other virgins, saying, Lord, Lord, open to us. But he answered and said, Verily I say unto you, I know you not. <u>Matthew 25:2-12</u>

One cannot credibly deny that a distinct separation is made of the virgins based on one simple thing. Some had oil, and some did not! Furthermore, those who had oil were somehow connected with "knowing" and "being known" by our Lord, and the others without the oil were not "known" by our Lord. Everything in this parable deserves our utmost attention and needs our deepest scrutiny in order to understand what Jesus was conveying to us, but one thing stands indisputably clear; at the end of the age there is going to be a separation between some of the Lord's saints and the rest. This separation is inevitable and will be determined by things totally within the control of the saints themselves. Thus the admonition given by Jesus at the end of the parable: *Watch therefore, for ye know neither the day nor the hour wherein the Son of man cometh.* This is the same admonition that Luke recorded in his Gospel… *Watch and Pray that ye may be counted worthy to escape…*

There are more accounts in the New Testament pointing to this coming separation between the wise and the foolish, but if these are not enough to capture your heart, it's doubtful that more evidence will convince you, thus sealing the coming fate with destiny as a person who should have known the truth and the time of visitation but was instead... BLINDSIDED

A New Look

Is it possible? Is it possible to hold a view of the book of Revelation that fits together with every other scripture that addresses "end-time" issues? For years, I have struggled with the statements recorded in the Bible that contradict the popular end-time scenarios advocated by so many.

For example: Popular scenarios suggest that Revelation Chapter 4 depicts the rapture of the church when John is invited to come up into heaven.

After this I looked, and, behold, a door was opened in heaven: and the first voice which I heard was as it were of a trumpet talking with me; which said, Come up hither, and I will shew thee things which must be hereafter. <u>Revelation 4:1</u>

Was God only inviting John up into heaven in order to show him future events, or was this representative of the entire church at the rapture? The "rapture" interpretation seems to be an appropriate application, until we read something later in chapter 6. There we read about an astounding event described below.

And I beheld when he had opened the sixth seal, and, lo, there was a great earthquake; and the sun became black as sackcloth of hair, and the moon became as blood; And the stars of heaven fell unto the earth, even as a fig tree casteth her untimely figs·, when she is shaken of a mighty wind. And the heaven departed as a scroll when it is rolled together; and every mountain and island were moved out of their places. <u>Revelation 6:12-14</u>

According to popular belief, the rapture of the church [chapter 4] happens before this great display of terrible disruption [chapter 6]. But, when we read Jesus' own description in Matthew of the very same events, we get an entirely different schedule of the rapture of the church.

Immediately after the tribulation of those days shall the sun be darkened, and the moon shall not give her light, and the stars shall fall from heaven, and the powers of the heavens shall be shaken: Matthew 24: 29

__And then__ shall appear the sign of the Son of man in heaven: and then shall all the tribes of the earth mourn, and they shall see the Son of man coming in the clouds of heaven with power and great glory. And he shall send his angels with a great sound of a trumpet, and they shall gather together his elect from the four winds, from one end of heaven to the other. Matthew 24: 30-31

It seems that Jesus is declaring the rapture of his church will follow the "sun, moon, stars, and earthquake" event. At that time, he gathers his elect from every point on the planet, and from every place in heaven. Added to this seeming discrepancy are some other words of Jesus recorded in Luke.

And there shall be signs in the sun, and in the moon, and in the stars; and upon the earth distress of nations, with perplexity; the sea and the waves roaring; Men's hearts failing them for fear, and for looking after those things which are coming on the earth: for the powers of heaven shall be shaken. __And then__ shall they see the Son of man coming in a cloud with power and great glory. And when these things begin to come to pass, then look up, and lift up your heads; for your redemption draweth nigh. Luke 21:25-28

Here again Jesus specifically places our redemption after the sun, moon, and stars event! Is it possible to have an understanding of end times that incorporates every available scripture addressing the issue? Surely God's word is not in contradiction to itself. Yet, even some of Paul's writings add to the seeming discrepancy.

Behold, I shew you a mystery; We shall not all sleep, but we shall all be changed, In a moment, in the twinkling of an eye, __at the last trump__: for the trumpet __shall sound__, and the dead shall be raised incorruptible, and we shall be changed. I Corinthians 15:51-52

7

Paul emphatically announces the redemption of our bodies to be at the last trumpet. Anyone who has read the book of Revelation readily sees that it is blown in Chapter 11. There is no mention of a trumpet blowing ever again after Chapter 11 in the book of Revelation, or the bible.

And the <u>seventh angel sounded</u>; and there were great voices in heaven, saying, The kingdoms of this world are become the kingdoms of our Lord, and of his Christ; and he shall reign for ever and ever. And the four and twenty elders, which sat before God on their seats, fell upon their faces, and worshipped God, Saying, We give thee thanks, O Lord God Almighty, which art, and wast, and art to come; because thou hast taken to thee thy great power, and hast reigned. And the nations were angry, and thy wrath is come, and <u>the time of the dead, that they should be judged, and that thou shouldest give reward</u> unto thy servants the prophets, and to the saints, and them that fear thy name, small and great; and shouldest destroy them which destroy the earth. <u>Revelation 11:15-18</u>

And how do we incorporate Paul's warning to the Church recorded in the book of Thessalonians:

Now we beseech you, brethren, by the coming of our Lord Jesus Christ, and by our gathering together unto him… Let no man deceive you by any means: for that day shall not come, except there come a falling away first, and that man of sin be revealed…
<u>II Thessalonians 2:1-3</u>

Paul seems to make a point blank assertion that a great falling away from the faith will occur and the antichrist will be here in power before the coming of Christ and our gathering together to him.

Perhaps we need a new look at the time table God has so wisely and graciously given to us. It is, after all, his idea, and his plan to give us a look into the unfolding of events:

And I heard, but I understood not: then said I, O my Lord, what shall be the end of these things? And he said, Go thy way, Daniel:

for the words are closed up and sealed till the time of the end. Many shall be purified, and made white, and tried; but the wicked shall do wickedly: and none of the wicked shall understand; but the wise shall understand. Daniel 12:8-10

CHRONOLOGY

There is a wide, wide variety of interpretations given to the words of the book of Revelation, or as some refer to it… the Apocalypse. Perhaps one of the biggest reasons we find so many interpretations is directly attributable to the lack of proper chronology assigned to the book. For an example, if we wanted to describe "your day", we might list the events of your day on a piece of paper in chronological order. Then, anyone reading your list would get a pretty accurate understanding of how your day unfolded. It might look something like this:

Woke up
Got out of bed
Stumbled to the bathroom
Showered
Dressed
Fixed Hair
Made Coffee
Grabbed some cereal
Brushed teeth
Put on Coat & Boots
Went to the Garage
Started Car
Opened Garage Door
Backed out
Drove to work
Etc. etc.

Your list might be more or less detailed, but one could readily grasp the reality of your day. Now, suppose you wanted several people to understand and grasp how your day unfolded, but somehow the list got scrambled up and the chronological order of the above events got changed for each person. You not only would leave a lot of people confused, but also you would leave them without much comprehension of your day. The more people you gave the scrambled lists, the greater the disagreement would be about what you did that day. The scenarios might be fun, but of little value about the credible events of your day. Perhaps a list one person might receive would look like this:

Went to the Garage
Showered
Backed out
Woke up
Opened Garage Door
Fixed Hair
Put on Coat & Boots
Grabbed some cereal
Drove to work
Made Coffee
Brushed teeth
Started the car
Stumbled to the Bathroom
Got out of bed
Dressed
Etc. etc.

Not only would each person be "confused" concerning your day, but depending on the particular list they got, there would be a big disagreement between any two of them as to the events of your day. Each weird list might require people to "leave out" some of the things you wrote and others to greatly "twist" the meaning of what you wrote in order for things to make a little bit of logical sense.

In many ways, this is what has happened to the book of Revelation. One of the greatest hindrances to comprehending the book has been the lack of chronology; or better yet, the lack of a biblical chronology. It's easy to see why we have at least 666 interpretations for the book of Revelation. Many of the authors who have written upon the subject have ignored the biblical chronology intrinsic in the book and substituted their own subjective chronology. The results have been total confusion and mayhem for people interested in what it says. In fact, the most common response to the book of Revelation has been something like this:

"I believe it's God's inspired word, but it's too controversial, and divisive, and too hard for me to grasp. There are just too many interpretations. For me, the most important message is to realize that God wins, and I need to be ready for the coming of the Lord Jesus."

Frankly, I fully understand how the majority of people feel! I too, am overwhelmed by the variety of interpretations given to the book. How is the average, common, believer who works 40 hours a week, manages a household, attends at least twelve functions a month, and is attempting to guide a Christian family through a corrupt world, supposed to sort out anything of value from the book of Revelation when even the "experts" can't agree on what it means?

However, I'm also fully convinced of another reality as well. Not only do I believe God is the author of the book, but that the book was given with purpose, and meaning for the child of God. I believe God gave not only incredible information about the end of the age, but also some very valuable, and vital information to the children of God who would be alive at the time of its fulfillment. I cannot believe in my heart that God would record with such detail so many astounding things and not intend for his people to grasp what it foretells, and what it all means! He simply does not waste time on foolishness. The book of Revelation even includes threats of woe upon people who would alter its content; and declares blessings upon those who treasure its statements. No other book in the entire Bible is given with such pronouncements of woe and blessing. What does God so earnestly want to reveal to the average believer at the end of the age? If you are compelled, as I am, to discover what treasures God has recorded in the book of Revelation, please accept this one tiny bit of advice offered in the spirit of meekness and hope that you will find out what God is saying to you. Discover what chronology God has given the book, and never depart from it for any reason!

We teachers of the Book of Revelation often present fascinating ideas. We may come with worthy motives and even reasonable logic; but if we stray the least bit from God's given chronology, then a whole arena of confusion is opened up for the sincere student of prophecy. Furthermore, this can lead to a twisting, bending, or ignoring of certain parts of God's word in order to maintain a sensible logic in the scenarios presented by the teacher. This warning about teachers of Revelation is not given to disparage the sincere efforts of any person trying to convey the book of Revelation to another. God knows it's a book of symbolism and metaphor, swirling through many different timeframes and places in our universe, both spiritual and natural; making it a most difficult subject to address. However, this does emphasize the necessity of a pure "biblical chronology" and reminds us how indispensable it is to our research and understanding of the book! Proper chronology is the absolute bedrock upon which any serious student must begin building his or her understanding of God's revelation about the end of the age. Any other approach will ultimately end in some form of error and confusion for the student of the Bible.

So, what is "biblical chronology", you might ask? Is there disagreement about "biblical chronology" as well? Indeed, there is a plethora of chronologies espoused by various teachers of Revelation. How does one determine what "biblical chronology" really is? Let me point out some self-evident revelations God has given us, and allow you to evaluate the validity of these revelations as they pertain to chronology. I'm not interested in spending half of the pages of this book verifying and defending my position on the correct "biblical chronology" presented in the book of Revelation. Instead, let me refer you to some common sense ideas.

Do you think an author on the New York Times Best Seller List would put forth a book in which a normal reader could not readily discern the chronology of his/her story? I think not! If a book looked like one of those scrambled lists of your day's events [mentioned earlier], it would never make the best seller list, because no one could comprehend it. There would be no compelling reason to purchase a book that made no sense. In like manner, I dare say, God has given us a book whose chronology can quite readily be discerned. We are not looking for some lost code, or some magical key to discern the chronology of the book of Revelation. I, for one, believe God when He declared it to be an open book.

Then he instructed me, "Do not seal up the prophetic words you have written, for the time is near." Revelation 22:10 [NLT]

With this in mind, allow me to point you to some very, self-evident, biblical chronology in the book of Revelation. If you are not very familiar with the book, then of course, you may not be familiar with some of the following facts, but even a summary reading of the book will clearly show the following demarcations.

Chapters 2-4 are composed of information both actual and symbolic clustered about **Seven Churches**.

Chapters 5-7 are composed of information both actual and symbolic clustered about a scroll with **Seven Seals**.

Chapters 8-14 are composed of information both actual and symbolic clustered about **Seven Trumpets**.

Chapter 15-18 is composed of information both actual and symbolic clustered about **Seven vials**.

These four sets of seven things are given in this specific order and follow chronologically one after the other. May I suggest to the common-sense person, that this is God's simple and clear chronology for the unfolding of his revelation of end time events? Not only are they given in this order, but are divided into chapters that follow a numerical chronology. To deviate from this layout, leads one into a wilderness of confusion. You might be thinking, "Well, what's so difficult about that?" The truth is, some modern-day teachers and authors ignore this very simple, "biblical chronology", relying instead upon a self-manipulated or re-arranged order of events in order to fit a preconceived notion of fulfillment; sometimes using it to interpret something that has happened in the world of current events that seem to match a certain verse in the book of Revelation.

Recently, I was given a monthly newsletter from a nationally recognized, and reputable, mainline, denominational ministry which hosts seminars and regional meetings on the topic of the End Times. The article was printed on high quality paper listing the radio and T.V. stations carrying their program. To my utter amazement, I read the unabashed interpretation of Revelation chapter 9. Saddam Hussein, former head of Iraq, [now deceased] was the supposed fulfillment of the character portrayed in verse 11.

And they had a king over them, which is the angel of the bottomless pit, whose name in the Hebrew tongue is Abaddon, but in the Greek tongue hath his name Apollyon. Revelation 9:11

On the surface, this may seem to be an appropriate and logical application; after all, the name Abaddon, or Apollyon means "destroyer". This may be a very fitting description of Saddam for many people across the world today. However, anyone who has made even a cursory reading of the book, realizes that this character mentioned in Revelation 9 is a character depicted during the timeframe of the 5th Trumpet. Chapter 9 begins with these words:

And the fifth angel blew his trumpet, and I saw a star fallen from heaven to earth, and he was given the key to the shaft of the bottomless pit. Revelation 9:1

If Saddam Hussein was actually the fulfillment of Revelation 9:11 then everything that is portrayed by the Seven Churches, the Seven Seals, and the Four preceding Trumpets, would already be fulfilled as well! And yet, according to this ministry's own teaching, many of those things have not yet been fulfilled. As you can see, this ministry makes up the chronology of Revelation in a very subjective and haphazard manner. If every teacher did this according to their own taste; then the results would be a completely different interpretation for every person taking up the task of interpreting the book! In some cases, this is exactly what has happened. Not only have many erroneous teachings come from such practice, but multitudes of Christians who ought to be blessed and enriched by God's Revelation, are instead vexed, frustrated, and jaded about the prospect of studying the book of Revelation. Whole denominations, fed-up with the turmoil, have given a token blessing to one particular interpretation and left it at that! Subject Closed!

Do we need any more evidence of how crucial it is to have a standard chronology, depicted by scripture itself, in order to perceive anything at all from God's marvelous truth given to the Church by the apostle John? I think not.

Consider these five points:

1. Surely we can assume that 99% of preachers, teachers, and authors dealing with the book of Revelation would be considered "rationally-minded" people.
2. All rationally thinking people would unanimously agree that God has conveyed only one, single chronology in the book of Revelation; all others falling short of the correct chronology intended by Him.
3. Any chronology aside from the one intended by God would not convey the precise knowledge available to the Saints.
4. Has God left us with the monumental task of determining which person he has "chosen" and "anointed" and given "special" "secret" "guidance" for declaring the real and true chronology of the events in Revelation?
5. God forbid! Let us rest upon the premise that the single, true chronology for the unfolding of Revelation events lies upon the printed text in our Bible…simply as it is written!

May God give us the wisdom to see the absolute need for his chronology in the story communicated by Revelation! Put aside all of your preconceived ideas garnered from your friends, your pastors, your denominational creeds, and simply listen to what is written! You may be surprised at what you see, but you will be incredibly secure in your position as you begin to see, not only Revelation, but a whole array of scriptures fit together in one clear, concise, and united revelation without any discrepancies. If you're ready, then why not walk up to God's Word and see *what is written*.

STAGING

Another devastating blow to understanding the book of Revelation is "staging". As confusing as scrambled chronologies have made the book of Revelation, we are now going to look at something that has caused just as many, maybe even more people, to veer off into the swamps of conflict and confusion. Turn your attention with me to the issue of "staging" for a moment. You may be wondering what staging has to do with interpreting the book of Revelation. Let me say it frankly, that mis-staging may contribute more to contradictions in the book of Revelation, than any other single issue.

Let's use a "stage play" as an example. If we were to attend a play of practically any kind, we would be seated in front of a stage of some sort, where players [actors] would portray for us a drama. On the stage would be props and scenes, [perhaps on backdrops], to help make the play more enjoyable and realistic to our minds. We've all seen them, from the most amateur to the exquisite, and detailed. Some plays even have "scene changes". The curtain drops and a new stage is prepared carrying the story and the viewers to an entirely different setting. This is all normal and really quite helpful in the telling of the story. Now, suppose someone set up the wrong stage for a particular scene. It could be laughable, or downright confusing to the viewer; a jail cell for a scene supposed to be carried on in a church; a background of the sea for a scene of someone trapped in the desert; a big city background in a play meant to be enacted in the country. You can let your imagination visualize a thousand different scenarios where the staging doesn't match the storyline. And yet this is exactly what sometimes occurs in the relaying of the message of Revelation. So much is built around a stage scene that may not even fit with the story. "How so", you may ask?

Let me begin by bringing up a familiar phrase to those engaged in studying the book of Revelation: "The seven year tribulation" or "The seven years of great tribulation". Aside from a handful of theologians no one even knows where this phrase came from. If you doubt that, ask around and see how many people can tell you where the idea of a seven year tribulation comes from. If you do find someone who quotes you a verse from the Old Testament, ask them to give you a clear, concise explanation of "how" they interpret that to mean "the seven year tribulation" or "The Great Tribulation". You are inviting to yourself quite an amusing challenge, to say the least.

You may already be aware of the fact there is no mention of a seven year tribulation period anywhere in the Bible. You may not be a Bible scholar and therefore have no idea if there is or not. It would be quite a chore to sit down and read the entire Bible with the single purpose of finding all the verses that talk about the seven year tribulation. If you would like to make it much easier, simply go to a Strong's Exhaustive Concordance, or another one of your choice, and look up either the word "seven" or "tribulation". These concordances have every listing of every word alphabetically, and you will readily discover that there is no verse in the Bible that refers to such an event. Instead, teachers have "deducted" that such a seven year tribulation is implied because of previous statements made in the Bible.
[We'll look into the validity of this "deduction" in a minute]

The point I would make at this juncture is that the widest held views on the book of Revelation rest upon a stage where the props and backdrop are made around a seven year period of tribulation. The most popular authors, film-makers, preachers, and teachers on the subject of Revelation, use a "seven year tribulation period" as the stage for all that is recorded in the book of Revelation. If the Bible does indeed imply that there is a seven year tribulation at the end of the age, then this staging is appropriate and useful in displaying the book of Revelation. If, however, there is no such thing implied in scripture, then unfolding Revelation's story with the props, and background of a non-existent seven year timeframe could be the cause of much misunderstanding, twisting, turning, and downright contradiction of God's own word. So, why do I even bring up the possibility that there might not be a seven year tribulation implied in scripture? Let's look at God's own record!

IT IS WRITTEN

As we view scripture and look at the popular description of end times, we can't help but take notice of various concerns. Primarily, we wonder how a "7 year Tribulation" ever came to be incorporated into popular belief. The book of Revelation itself, never mentions a 7 year time frame associated with any tribulation period. The whole of the New Testament never mentions a 7 year timeframe associated with anything. Indeed, the entire Bible does not make reference to a 7 year tribulation time frame at all.

So, we wonder, how it is that practically every description of end-time events is couched in a 7 year timeframe. Where does the idea come from; and how is it justified in scripture? Much is made of a verse in Daniel chapter 9 which we will address momentarily; but even Daniel only mentions a 3 ½ year timeframe for events revealed about the end time. This is described by using the word "time", "times", and "half", or [one time, two times, and ½ time].

And he shall speak great words against the most High, and shall wear out the saints of the most High, and think to change times and laws: and they shall be given into his hand until a time and times and the dividing of time. Daniel 7:25

And I heard the man clothed in linen, which was upon the waters of the river, when he held up his right hand and his left hand unto heaven, and sware by him that liveth for ever that it shall be for a time, times, and an half; and when he shall have accomplished to scatter the power of the holy people, all these things shall be finished. Daniel 12:7

On both of these occasions, only a 3 ½ year time frame is addressed while disclosing events prior to the time of Christ's return. In like manner, the book of Revelation only makes reference to a 3 ½ year time frame for specific events at the end of time, instead of a 7 year period.

And I will give power unto my two witnesses, and they shall prophesy a thousand two hundred and threescore days clothed in sackcloth. Revelation Chapter 11   [1,260 days = 3 ½ years]

And the woman fled into the wilderness, where she hath a place prepared of God, that they should feed her there a <u>thousand two hundred and threescore days</u>.   Revelation Chapter 12

And to the woman were given two wings of a great eagle, that she might fly into the wilderness, into her place, where she is nourished for a <u>time, and times, and half a time</u>, from the face of the serpent. <u>Revelation Chapter 12</u>

And there was given unto him a mouth speaking great things and blasphemies; and power was given unto him to continue <u>forty and two months</u>.   Revelation Chapter 13   [42 months= 3 ½ years]

So, what are we to make of these things recorded in the Bible when we see and hear so much teaching that does not seem to fit with God's revealed truth?   Is it possible to see clearly those things God has spoken in a plain presentation… a presentation in which every scripture aligns perfectly with every other scripture on the subject? I say emphatically, YES!...that is, if one wants to know truth;   that is if one wants to see truth regardless of what men may say on the subject;   that is if one is like Jesus in his defense against the attacks of His arch enemy.   Jesus triumphed gloriously by standing on a simple premise:

IT   IS   WRITTEN

Regretfully, it appears that a majority of God's children today are not particularly interested in understanding the book of Revelation. For some, it's simply too complicated.   For others, the contradictory views tossed about are overwhelming to the mind. And for many, it just seems like a whole lot of bother over unexplainable symbolism that cannot be made relevant to the everyday struggle merely to live in this modern, high-speed world. There are bills to pay, schedules to meet, relationships to handle, and far too many other time-consuming events crammed into everyday life, for people to personally research the book for themselves. It's so much simpler to put our stamp of approval on the interpretation pre-approved by our denominational organization and move on with life. A common attitude is couched in the phrase: "Well...we may not understand what it means, but as long as we are ready when Jesus comes, it will be alright."

In a general sense, that is true. But, we need to consider God's perspective for giving us the book. Why did He record things in such detail and refer to them in both the old and new testaments? Is it possible that vital information is prepared for his own people? Is it possible that our welfare depends on this information? Would God waste words on something that was not vitally important to his children? The angel that appeared to Daniel seems to indicate that the "wise" person will find a way to understand these things.

And many of them that sleep in the dust of the earth shall awake, some to everlasting life, and some to shame and everlasting contempt.... But thou, O Daniel, shut up the words, and seal the book, even to the time of the end: .... And he said,
Go thy way, Daniel: for the words are closed up and sealed till the time of the end. ...and none of the wicked shall understand; but the wise shall understand. Daniel 12: 2, 4, 9, 10

Should Christians today be content with the cavalier attitude of the average busy man on the street? Was Jesus referring to this mind-set when he foretold his coming would be at a time like the flood, when people were eating, drinking, and marrying, yet unaware and unprepared for the approaching catastrophe? Is there a certain preparedness that Jesus was urging for those who would be living at the time of the end? Is it alright for a Christian to simply "opt out" of a diligent pursuit of what has been recorded for our benefit? Will busy Christians one day regret that they simply accepted the popular beliefs held by their denomination, trusted preacher, or close friends? Truly, the wise will push past all of these things and approach the Word of God with vigor and an open heart and mind. After all, "the wise" are those who seek Him.

Maybe this is why Jesus shared the parable about the five wise and five foolish virgins to describe the conditions of the end time and his subsequent re-appearing.

Then shall the kingdom of heaven be likened unto ten virgins, which took their lamps, and went forth to meet the bridegroom. And five of them were wise, and five were foolish…And while they went to buy, the bridegroom came; and they that were ready went in with him to the marriage: and the door was shut. Matthew 25: 1, 10-12

For as a snare shall it come on all them that dwell on the face of the whole earth. Watch ye therefore, and pray always, that ye may be accounted worthy to escape all these things that shall come to pass, and to stand before the Son of man. Luke 21:35-36

If you are one of those who takes seriously the injunctions of Christ on this matter, then let me invite you to take a whole ***new look*** at a book that has confused many, and has become a closed subject in the minds of many others who need it's message the most! Are you ready to stand on the premise, "it is written"? If so, then strap on your seatbelt, gather up your courage, and let's look at what is written. Join me for a journey through the pages of God's revealed truth; keeping our eyes always upon this sole fact:

IT   IS   WRITTEN!

WHAT 7 YEAR TRIBULATION?

Perhaps the greatest stumbling block to understanding the book of Revelation is the commonly held assumption that the events described in the book, somehow fit into or around a final 7 year period known as the Great Tribulation. This assumption is so widespread, that virtually no book, article, sermon, tape, video, movie or C.D. suggests any other setting but the 7 years for the unfolding events described in Revelation. Tragically, no such time-frame is ever mentioned in the Bible! Therefore every effort to make things fit into this arbitrary setting, forces the diligent student to deal with verses and issues in a likewise arbitrary fashion. The results are mind-numbing. Serious seekers end up holding to a make-shift theory that simply does not accommodate all the various scriptures on the subject. Each candidate ends up "accepting" a certain theory they can live with, and then simply "dumping" those scriptures that don't fit into the acceptable interpretation. What else can they do??

A good understanding of God's revelation to us about the end of time is lost because of these two basic errors:
1. Neglecting scriptural chronology
2. Assuming a 7 year time-frame

The outcomes of such errors are self-evident. The interpretations cannot bear up under scrutiny without manipulating God's revealed chronology, and so one simply ignores relevant parts of "what is written". This need not be!

A third error, commonly accepted, works hand-in-hand with the supposed 7 year Tribulation. Unfortunately, it too adds clouds of confusion to our understanding as well; and yet it is one of the most widely accepted "beliefs" about the end-time scenario. This is the teaching about antichrist's 7 year treaty with Israel that he supposedly breaks midway through. The fog of confusion this doctrine has laid over God's testimony is staggering; and yet it is one of the most widely accepted and popular expectations of all Christendom. And so, God's "revelation" lies passively dormant under the darkness of these three widely held assumptions:

1. Neglecting scriptural chronology
2. Assuming a 7 year time-frame
3. Aligning events around a supposed broken treaty with Israel

Where did these ideas originate & how?

Probably most Christians think that the 7 year Tribulation and the 7 year rule of the antichrist are nothing less than orthodox teachings of the church. A little research will show you that the teaching was not even introduced until the 1500's by a Catholic Priest named Francisco Ribera, a Jesuit priest of Salamanca, in 1585. It was not until 200 years later that the Protestant church ever began to adhere to this doctrine. During the great Revival period beginning in the 1700's a popular Evangelist Rev. Darby came to adopt this aberrant doctrine as gospel. Although I don't mean to judge the man's integrity, it none-the-less helped lead to a great deception being foisted upon many an innocent layman.

Perhaps the reason for such a widespread acceptance of these teachings is due directly to some popular Bibles that began to be published and dispersed among an overwhelming number of Christians. They were the Scofield Study Bible, and also Dake's study Bible. These authors, among others, stimulated a burgeoning growth in the study of God's Word. The two Bibles included in their notes, a presentation of Revelation incorporating the aberrant teachings of the Catholic Priest, Riviera. It's been reported that Clarence Larkin has admitted that the material he got for his prophetic charts came from Francisco Ribera. Soon, the ideas fostered by the Priest were considered to be genuine orthodoxy by an overwhelming number of believers. The more it was taught and declared, the more it became entrenched into the dogma of many a professing Christian believer and Christian organization. It wasn't long before Bible Schools and Seminaries began turning out a host of ministers who innocently propagated the same underlying fallacies started by the priest four hundred years earlier. Today, these teachings serve as the very bedrock for interpreting the book of Revelation and other scriptures that deal with the end of the age. And now with the advent of television, movies, home video equipment, and "pop-culture" Christian literature, one can hardly get an audience long enough to expose the error that is blinding our eyes to vital, relevant truth for today!

All that one needs to remove the blinders and see the truth, is one serious look at a small passage in Daniel Chapter 9. For it is upon this one, single passage [indeed, one verse] that all of the aforementioned errors find their roots. It is this single text which has subverted the intelligent comprehension of the treasures given to us by our God in the book of Revelation. In fact, it is perhaps religious academia's worst failure in all of biblical study, because it undercuts one of hermeneutics' main principles by establishing an entire doctrine based upon one, single, solitary verse. Not only is establishing doctrine on one verse severely rebuked by religious academia, but the rule is used repeatedly to deny so much other heresy taught from scriptures. And yet, no other scripture is ever provided as verification of the doctrine taught from Daniel Chapter nine. Why then, do teachers and preachers continue to overlook this rule about establishing doctrine when it comes to Daniel Chapter nine? Perhaps it is time to stand on the simple premise:

IT IS WRITTEN

LET'S LOOK AT WHAT is WRITTEN

And whiles I was speaking, and praying, and confessing my sin and the sin of my people Israel, and presenting my supplication before the LORD my God for the holy mountain of my God, Yea, whiles I was speaking in prayer, even the man Gabriel, whom I had seen in the vision at the beginning, being caused to fly swiftly, touched me about the time of the evening oblation. And he informed me, and talked with me, and said, O Daniel, I am now come forth to give thee skill and understanding. At the beginning of thy supplications the commandment came forth, and I am come to shew thee; for thou art greatly beloved: therefore understand the matter, and consider the vision. Daniel 9:20-23

God wanted to reveal some things to Daniel, His greatly beloved servant. Gabriel, himself, was dispatched to do the honors. Pay close attention to what is written.

A period of seventy sets of seven has been decreed for your people and your holy city to put down rebellion, to bring an end to sin, to atone for guilt, to bring in everlasting righteousness, to confirm the prophetic vision, and to anoint the Most Holy ...
Daniel 9:24   *[The New Living Translation]*

Seventy weeks are determined upon thy people and upon thy holy city, to finish the transgression, and to make an end of sins, and to make reconciliation for iniquity, and to bring in everlasting righteousness, and to seal up the vision and prophecy, and to anoint the most Holy.

The KJV uses the term "seventy weeks" instead of "seventy sets of seven". The concordance uses "sevens" not "weeks" as the meaning. Many scholars agree with the use of the word "sevens".

Notice upon whom this decree is given. God has decreed seventy sets of seven [or 490 years] upon the Jews, Daniel's people; and upon Jerusalem, the holy city. Don't forget this. It is very important to understanding what God is declaring. We will soon find that this is an ultimatum for the Jewish nation, now being presented to Daniel. At the end of the 490 year probation, the time for God's judgment will have reached the apex. Please carefully note that six things will be fulfilled within the 490 year time period. We will soon see that these six things end God's patience with the rebellious nation of Judah.

Now listen and understand! Seven sets of seven plus sixty-two sets of seven pass from the time the command is given to rebuild Jerusalem until the Anointed One. Jerusalem will be rebuilt with streets and strong defenses, in the perilous times. Daniel 9: 25 (NLT)

Know therefore and understand, that from the going forth of the commandment to restore and to build Jerusalem unto the Messiah

26

the Prince shall be seven weeks, and threescore and two weeks: the street shall be built again, and the wall, even in troublous times.

The angel indicated 69 sets of sevens would pass. We would say "483 years would pass". In our language and concepts, he is saying: "483 years from the time the commandment is given to rebuild Jerusalem…the Messiah will come." We know him as the Christ, Jesus, the only begotten son of God. So, when Jesus arrived as the anointed one, 69 of the 70 sets of seven are gone. At that time there is only one set of seven left in the prophesied time-frame. Or, as we would say, "7 more years" left for the prophecy to be completed. So, 7 years remained from Jesus' presentation to the Jews by John the Baptist until the probation was over.

After this period of sixty-two sets of seven , the Anointed One will be killed, appearing to have accomplished nothing, and a ruler will arise whose armies will destroy the city and the Temple. The end will come with a flood, and war and its miseries are decreed from that time to the very end. Daniel 9:26 [NLT]

And after (the) threescore and two weeks shall Messiah be cut off, but not for himself: and the people of the prince that shall come shall destroy the city and the sanctuary; and the end thereof shall be with a flood, and unto the end of the war desolations are determined.

Here's where diversion from truth begins. Liberties are taken with the interpretation in order to fit the pre-supposed theory of the modern translators who view this "ruler" as the coming antichrist. The original clearly states that **the people of the prince that shall come will destroy the city and temple.** This coming prince could be determined to be Caesar, or his General, Titus; but it cannot be the antichrist, as we will soon see. I invite you to take a closer look at who this coming prince is! It's also possible that the coming prince is the very same **coming prince** that is in the previous verse 25. It could be **Messiah the Prince**. The Catholic Priest, Ribera is the one who first misapplied this scripture to mean the antichrist instead of the Christ, or Titus, etc. As you will see, further verses make it even clearer that the **coming Prince** cannot be the antichrist.

Jesus made it clear in the New Testament that it was the rejection by the Jews [the people of the Prince] that was bringing destruction down upon the City, the Temple, and the Nation. Jesus wept over Jerusalem, lamenting that they recognized neither their Prince, nor the visitation of judgment coming upon them. God's time clock of 490 years was drawing to a close to "**put down rebellion, to bring an end to sin, to atone for guilt, to bring in everlasting righteousness, to confirm the prophetic vision, and to anoint the Most Holy** ".

Here again the modern translators move into preconceived ideas based on their belief that this text refers to the antichrist who will make a "treaty" with the Jews for 7 years. They further believe that he will break his treaty after 3 ½ years by setting up a sacrilegious object in the Temple. Look at the following translation.

He will make a treaty with the people for a period of one set of seven, but after half this time, he will put an end to the sacrifices and offerings. Then as a climax to all his terrible deeds, he will set up a sacrilegious object that causes desecration, until the end that has been decreed is poured out on this defiler. Daniel 9:27 [NLT]

And he shall confirm the covenant with many for one week: and in the midst of the week he shall cause the sacrifice and the oblation to cease, and for the overspreading of abominations he shall make it desolate, even until the consummation, and that determined shall be poured upon the desolate. Daniel 9:27

I call your attention to what is written. In the first place it is a **covenant** that is **confirmed** [strengthened and made firm] for 7 years, not a treaty that is "made". Furthermore, it is not just any covenant, but **THE COVENANT** which is confirmed. Please read what Jeremiah said about The Covenant:

Behold, the days come, saith the LORD, that I will make a new covenant with the house of Israel, and with the house of Judah: Not according to the covenant that I made with their fathers in the day that I took them by the hand to bring them out of the land of Egypt; which my covenant they brake, although I was an husband unto them, saith the LORD: But this shall be the covenant that I will make with the house of Israel; After those days, saith the LORD, I will put my law in their inward parts, and write it in their hearts; and will be their God, and they shall be my people. Jeremiah 31:31-33

Now read what Christ said on the night of his betrayal 3 ½ years after John announced him as the Messiah. [483 years + 3 ½ years] This was 486 ½ years after the commandment to build Jerusalem was made in 452 B.C.]

And in the same way He took the cup after they had eaten, saying, "This cup which is poured out for you is the new covenant *in My blood.*   Luke 22:20   [ASV]

Daniel 9:27 states that *in the midst of the week he shall cause the sacrifice and the oblation to cease* [to fail, put away, to rest].   As you recall, when Jesus was crucified on Golgotha's hill, the veil down at the Temple was rent top to bottom.   Jesus was the Lamb of God that was slain.   He concluded all sacrifices for sin and did away with the old sacrificial system, at least from God's perspective.   The book of Hebrews points that out quite effectively.

Then said I, Lo, I am come (In the roll of the book it is written of me) To do thy will, O God. Saying above, Sacrifices and offerings and whole burnt offerings and sacrifices for sin thou wouldest not, neither hadst pleasure therein (the which are offered according to the law), then hath he said, Lo, I am come to do thy will. He taketh away the first [sacrifice], *that he may establish the second* [sacrifice]. *By which will we have been sanctified through the offering of the body of Jesus Christ once for all.*   Hebrews 10:7-10

Again, I call your attention to what is written.   In the first place it is a **covenant** that is **confirmed** [strengthened and made firm] for 7 years, not a treaty.   Furthermore, it is not just any covenant, but **THE COVENANT** which is confirmed.   Now, add to this the fact that it is a covenant confirmed only for 7 years and only with the

JEWS [Daniel's people]. And add to this fact, that it is only confirmed with **many**… not all the Jews. So, a quick look at the book of Acts will reveal that *the word of God increased; and the number of the disciples multiplied in Jerusalem greatly; and a great company of the priests were obedient to the faith.* <u>Acts 6:7</u>

God, in Christ was confirming the Old Covenant with the Jews for the final seven years of the prophesied 490. But, in the end, Jesus was rejected by the leaders and the nation. And, in this same chapter we find Stephen becoming the first martyr of the young church. Not long after this in Chapter 10 we find a most amazing change occurring in the history of the Jewish world. By divine intervention and divine appointment, Peter is introduced to a brand new paradigm, and instructed to take the Gospel to the Gentiles at Cornelius' house, who then, are suddenly made partakers of the <u>New Covenant</u> without being or becoming Jewish! From that point onward, the New Testament shifts all the focus from the Jewish converts to the Gentile converts; from the old covenant, to the new covenant! Although we have no proof of the timing of the first gentile conversion, we know it was after Stephen was stoned by the Christ-rejecting Jews, and [I'm persuaded by Gabriel's prophecy] was 3 ½ years after Jesus' death. Thus the 490 year prophesied decree of Gabriel was fulfilled when God abandoned the unbelieving Nation of the Jews with its old covenant and initiated the New Covenant with the Gentiles. God, in Christ, fulfilled his message to Daniel precisely by confirming the old covenant with many of the Jews for 7 years; causing the old sacrifices for sin to fail in the midst of the 7 years; and then waiting three and one half more years before temporarily cutting off the unbelieving Jews and putting away the old covenant he had held with them for nearly 2,000 years.

Interestingly enough, the purveyors of the 7 year antichrist, and 7 year tribulation theory must resort to a most unusual means for changing the stated 490 year prophecy given by Gabriel to a 2490+ year fulfillment. This is easily accomplished by them, attributing something singular to this verse that is never applied to any other text in the entire Bible that declares an exact number of years. The interpreters merely insist that there is a huge "gap" between the first 483 years and the final 7 years which will no doubt, in their minds, be fulfilled at the end of the age. However, that interpretation begs the question: "is anything determined upon the Jews in the intervening years?" And, who determined that "God's prophetical time clock stopped?" We see this as manipulating the written word to coincide with a proposed theory. It would seem better to rest on "it is written" 490 years are determined!

Finally, in order to make the "gap theory" workable, it is also arbitrarily declared that those final 7 years will be the great tribulation, and that those final 7 years will be the time for antichrist's rule, in spite of the fact that Daniel himself only attributes 3 ½ years to his rule.

And the ten horns out of this kingdom are ten kings that shall arise: and another shall rise after them; and he shall be diverse from the first, and he shall subdue three kings. And he shall speak great words against the most High, and shall wear out the saints of the most High, and think to change times and laws: and they shall be given into his hand until a time and times and the dividing of time. *But the judgment shall sit, and they shall take away his dominion, to consume and to destroy it unto the end.*
Daniel 7: 24-26

This could be rendered [one time, two times, and ½ time] most writers agreeing that it means 3 ½ years. This 3 ½ year time-frame is confirmed in the book of Revelation.

And there was given unto him a mouth speaking great things and blasphemies; and power was given unto him to continue forty and two months. Revelation 13:5

Now, let's go back and see a final proof that the Prince that would come, cannot be a supposed anti-Christ at the end of the age. In review, the scripture states:

...and the people of the prince that shall come shall destroy the city and the sanctuary; and the end thereof shall be with a flood, and unto the end of the war desolations are determined. And he shall confirm the covenant with many for one week: and in the midst of the week he shall cause the sacrifice and the oblation to cease, and for the overspreading of abominations he shall make it desolate, even until the consummation, and that determined shall be poured upon the desolate. Daniel 9:26-27

Abominations did overspread the Jewish nation, and so God [and Christ seated on His throne with Him] made the city, the temple, indeed the entire country DESOLATE. A Roman General, Titus, was allowed by God to go and totally destroy the temple, the city, and the Jewish nation.

At very best, theologians could surmise that the coming prince was Titus. But, to make this "Prince" the future antichrist, simply will not hold up under scrutiny. Please read carefully what is written: *he shall make it desolate, even until the consummation* [utter riddance]

In 70 A.D. the City, State, and Temple of Judah were utterly destroyed! But, no such utter destruction is expected in Israel's future. Not a single theologian has described a total and utter riddance of Israel, Jerusalem, and its future temple during the rule of antichrist. In fact, the Bible declares the opposite in the book of Zechariah:

Behold, the day of the LORD cometh, and thy spoil shall be divided in the midst of thee. For I will gather all nations against Jerusalem to battle; and the city shall be taken, and the houses rifled, and the women ravished; and half of the city shall go forth into captivity, and the residue of the people shall not be cut off from the city. Then shall the LORD go forth, and fight against those nations, as when he fought in the day of battle. And his feet shall stand in that day upon the mount of Olives.
Zechariah 14: 1-4

Even a casual observer can see that this describes the future return of Jesus to Jerusalem at his second coming. In plain language, the Bible says there will be no utter, complete, and total riddance of Judah, the temple, and Jerusalem as it happened in 70 A.D. Therefore, the Prince described in Daniel 9 cannot be the coming antichrist; for he makes an utter riddance. Therefore, he is not the one who confirms the covenant with many for seven years. Therefore, he is not the one who breaks a supposed treaty in the middle of the seven years. Therefore, the prophecies of Jeremiah concerning the New Covenant stand affirmed by Gabriel in his declaration of what would transpire with the Jews.

One final piece of evidence that the 490 years have already transpired is the fact that all 6 of the proposed decrees were fulfilled by Christ:

Seventy weeks are determined upon thy people and upon thy holy city, to finish the transgression, and to make an end of sins, and to make reconciliation for iniquity, and to bring in everlasting righteousness, and to seal up the vision and prophecy, and to anoint the most Holy.   Daniel 9: 24

Take note of what is written:

1. Finish [restrict, restrain] the transgression [rebellion]
    But he was wounded for our transgressions   Isaiah 53:5
    That is why Jesus came to die.
2. To make an end of sins
    For it is impossible for the blood of bulls and goats to take away sins...For by a single offering he has perfected for all time those who are being sanctified.   Hebrews 10:4 & 14

3. To make reconciliation for iniquity
    God was in Christ, reconciling the world unto himself, not imputing their trespasses unto them.   II Corinthians 5:19

4. To bring in everlasting righteousness
    But now the righteousness of God without the law is

manifested, being witnessed by the law and the prophets; Even the righteousness of God which is by faith of Jesus Christ unto all and upon all them that believe. Romans 3:21-22

5. To seal up the vision and prophecy
    But those things, which God before had shewed by the mouth of all his prophets, that Christ should suffer, he hath so fulfilled. Acts 3:18

    Think not that I am come to destroy the law, or the prophets: I am not come to destroy, but to fulfill. Matthew 5:17

6. To anoint the most Holy
    The Spirit of the Lord is upon me, because he hath anointed me... Luke 4:18
    ...therefore also that holy thing which shall be born of thee shall be called holy—the Son of God. Luke 1:35

These are just the tip of the iceberg. A lot more New Testament verses could be quoted to establish these truths with many witnesses. The important issue is already shown. There is no such thing as a biblical declaration of a 7 year tribulation.

[This does not indicate that there is no such thing as a tribulation period; only that it is never limited to a 7 year time-frame dominated by the antichrist]. There is no such thing as a biblical declaration of a 7 year treaty between the Jews and a future antichrist. These are simply ideas foisted upon a gullible laity that has not researched what is written.

In the spirit of this understanding, one may now turn to the book of Revelation with a "clean slate" and begin to see what it declares about itself, rather than imposing a timeframe upon the book. If one is careful to apply the chronology given by the book, then he is ready to plunge forward into the Revelation, paying close attention to **what is written**!

THE SEVEN SEALS

The book of Revelation is nicely divided into 22 chapters. Our primary focus in this writing will be on chapters 6 through 19. These are the chapters that communicate to us the future developments in this world before the return of Christ with the commencement of His millennial reign upon the earth. For the sake of limiting this present work, we will not address the subject of Christ's messages to the seven churches contained within the first 3 chapters. Nor will we address the marvelous unfolding of God's plan for the earth beyond the time of Christ's millennial reign. It is these "in-between chapters" that present to the church a clear understanding of what God reveals to us about the way history will unfold during the final few years before His return.

We will look at "what is written" as it relates to the Seven Seals, the Seven Trumpets, and the Seven Bowls. Chapters 6 & 7 relay the information revealed by the seven seals. This is followed by Chapters 8-14 which relay the information revealed by the seven trumpets. And, finally, Chapters 15-19 follow and will relay information related to the seven bowls.

The first seal is broken by Jesus Christ in heaven. His simple act unleashes a flurry of activity upon the earth. One could say that the first seal opening actually begins the final years before the end of this world. It is the initial act of Christ bringing the kingdoms of this world down. It is the commencement of this world system's demise. Up until this moment in time, this world was allowed to follow the path of its choosing, and establish the desires of its own heart in accord with the Prince of this world, Satan. With the breaking of the first seal, God sets in motion a series of events; a count-down if you will, that will ultimately lead to Armageddon and the destruction of all that opposes or exalts itself against God. Keep in mind that the re-establishing of God's universal kingdom here on earth involves the overthrow of both physical and spiritual enemies. That is to say, the battle is waged in two arenas; the spiritual arena of Satan and his angels, and in the physical arena of man and his rebellious system of rule. Throughout the book of Revelation we will see these two arenas presented as a single entity, and rightly so. For, the dominion given to man by God was usurped by Satan himself long ago in the Garden of Eden. Unregenerate man, in his fallen nature, continues to hold authority in this world only in conjunction with the arch deceiver, Satan himself. This is why the nations and empires of this world are depicted in the book of Revelation as one body with Satan; as a beast with seven heads.

And I stood upon the sand of the sea, and saw a beast rise up out of the sea, having seven heads and ten horns, and upon his horns ten crowns, and upon his heads the name of blasphemy. And the beast which I saw was like unto a leopard, and his feet were as the feet of a bear, and his mouth as the mouth of a lion: and the dragon gave him his power, and his seat, and great authority.
Revelation 13:1-2

The imagery is stark, but the reality it projects is just as harsh. The dismantling and destruction of God's enemies is not a pretty sight. It is real, and will definitely entail much struggle, pain, sorrow, bloodshed, disease, starvation, horror, and war. Man and the god of this world will not yield easily to the fulfillment of the Saints' prayer… "thy kingdom come, thy will be done on earth as it is in heaven". It will require the intervention of God almighty before man and Satan will be forced to yield. But, yield they will! One set of scriptural imagery pictures a woman in travail, and "pained to be delivered". And, just as a woman experiences increasing spasms of pain and contraction before birth, so will the final few years of this world be with ever-increasing pressure from not only world governments, and not only from the physical elements surrounding us, and not only from the unseen spirit world controlling unregenerate man, but also from God almighty and His Christ who reigns in the earth.

And there will be strange events in the skies—signs in the sun, moon, and stars. And down here on earth the nations will be in turmoil, perplexed by the roaring seas and strange tides. The courage of many people will falter because of the fearful fate they see coming upon the earth, because the stability of the very heavens will be broken up. Luke 21:25-26 [NLT]

The good part in all of this is God's concern and care for His own. Jesus said: *But when these things begin to come to pass, look up, and lift up your heads; because your redemption draweth nigh.* Luke 21:28

With the opening of the first seal, the unavoidable, unstoppable. unchangeable march to Armageddon is begun.

And I saw when the Lamb opened one of the seals, and I heard, as it were the noise of thunder, one of the four beasts saying, Come and see. And I saw, and behold a white horse: and he that sat on him had a bow; and a crown was given unto him: and he went forth conquering, and to conquer. Revelation 6:1-2

Various opinions circulate as to who this conqueror might be or who he may represent. Some suggest Christ himself. Others believe it represents antichrist making his move to take over the world. Both views may be grounded on some solid logic. However, in light of current events of our own time, and in conjunction with other scriptural evidence put forth in Ezekiel 38 & 39, it is becoming increasingly plausible that this conqueror is none other than the Muslim religion itself, or the prophesied coming of the 12th Imam [Islamic spiritual leader]. I lean increasingly to this latter interpretation based on several facts.

First of all, the book of Revelation does not even introduce the antichrist kingdom until Chapter 13. Naturally, it follows, that this first seal more likely depicts someone other than antichrist. **Secondly,** I believe, like so many of my predecessors, that we are indeed very near to the close of the age. If in fact we are, then time itself throws the Muslim agenda into the forefront of world activity. **Thirdly**, it is the boasted religious goal of Islamic leaders to go forth conquering and to conquer, thereby achieving world conquest. **Fourthly,** the description of the next few seals reveals a world full of war, famine, disease, and slaughter followed by the unsealing of

37

the 6th seal. Like the proverbial last straw, the greatest and most dazzling prophecy ever foretold in the Bible suddenly erupts on our planet. And with it, the announcement of the great day of His wrath! This wrath of God has been prophesied for ages by the prophets of God. At long last, His long suffering comes to an abrupt and decisive end. There is nothing left but the unleashing of His wrath.

And I beheld when he had opened the sixth seal, and, lo, there was a great earthquake; and the sun became black as sackcloth of hair, and the moon became as blood; And the stars of heaven fell unto the earth, even as a fig tree casteth her untimely figs, when she is shaken of a mighty wind. And the heaven departed as a scroll when it is rolled together; and every mountain and island were moved out of their places. Revelation 6:12-14

Coincidentally, a similar event is described by Ezekiel which is forecast to take place in the latter times. The Ezekiel description is prophesied to be the reaction of God towards the invading Muslim armies. [without taking the time to prove these are Muslim countries, I stand on the names of the countries mentioned in the book of Ezekiel]

And it shall come to pass at the same time when Gog shall come against the land of Israel, saith the Lord GOD, that my fury shall come up in my face. For in my jealousy and in the fire of my wrath have I spoken, Surely in that day there shall be a great shaking in the land of Israel; So that the fishes of the sea, and the fowls of the heaven, and the beasts of the field, and all creeping things that creep upon the earth, and all the men that are upon the face of the earth, shall shake at my presence, and the mountains shall be thrown down, and the steep places shall fall, and every wall shall fall to the ground. Ezekiel 38:18-20

Not only does heaven and earth shake at the time of this Muslim invasion, but stuff falls out of the sky just like the events described by the 6th Seal.

And I will plead against him with pestilence and with blood; and I will rain upon him, and upon his bands, and upon the many people that are with him, an overflowing rain, and great hailstones, fire, and brimstone. <u>Ezekiel 38:22</u>

Meanwhile, back at the second seal; when Jesus breaks it, peace is taken from the earth. In a general sense, peace has never really dwelt on the earth since the fall of man. But in a real sense, the broken seal reminds us that nations have had times of peace in the past, but that luxury seems to come to an end with the breaking of the 2nd seal. This could well describe a world-wide Jihad expected by devout Muslims. Perhaps a perpetual wartime conflict will rage the remainder of the time left for the kingdoms of this world.

And when he had opened the second seal, I heard the second beast say, Come and see. And there went out another horse that was red: and power was given to him that sat thereon to take peace from the earth, and that they should kill one another: and there was given unto him a great sword. <u>Revelation 6:3-4</u>

The 3rd seal, is really no surprise at all, since "famine" and "inflation" are common consequences occurring during and after prolonged wars. If one could calculate the number of people who have died from an inadequate food supply due to the ravages of war, it would, no doubt be a staggering number. Even in our modern world, we witness the devastation of hunger on poor warring countries. As the world rushes to its certain destruction, an increasing number of lives will be lost to the horrors of starving to death, while others will face the plague of hyper-inflation, requiring a day's wages just to buy food for the day.

And when he had opened the third seal, I heard the third beast say, Come and see. And I beheld, and lo a black horse; and he that sat on him had a pair of balances in his hand. And I heard a voice in the midst of the four beasts say, A measure of wheat for a penny, and three measures of barley for a penny; <u>Revelation 6:5-6</u>

The toll is so high during the opening days of the end-time

judgments that it appears likely that ¼ of the population could be at risk of dying.

And when he had opened the fourth seal, I heard the voice of the fourth beast say, Come and see. And I looked, and behold a pale horse: and his name that sat on him was Death, and Hell followed with him. And power was given unto them over the fourth part of the earth, to kill with sword, and with hunger, and with death, and with the beasts of the earth. <u>Revelation 6:7-8</u>

Of course this description of the woe facing the planet could be interpreted to mean that a large number of people die, specifically within ¼ of the earth's area. It may be indicating an area of the planet that suffers the intensity of these wars. It could even refer to the area in conflict with the Muslim conqueror.

The breaking of the 5th seal unveils a curious development. The souls of dead people in heaven and near the altar of God are crying out to God for justice to be served on the earth. These are not simply souls of dead people, but the souls of those who had been martyred for Christ. They seem to hold a special right to restitution since their lives were cut short on the earth, specifically for their testimony of Christ.

And when he had opened the fifth seal, I saw under the altar the souls of them that were slain for the word of God, and for the testimony which they held: And they cried with a loud voice, saying, How long, O Lord, holy and true, dost thou not judge and avenge our blood on them that dwell on the earth? And white robes were given unto every one of them; and it was said unto them, that they should rest yet for a little season, until their fellowservants also and their brethren, that should be killed as they were, should be fulfilled. <u>Revelation 6:9-11</u>

The breaking of the 6th seal initiates what I call, the climactic, pivotal prophecy of the entire Bible. It is a prophecy issued by various prophets down through the ages, and is always given in association with the GREAT DAY OF THE LORD; or THE

GREAT DAY OF HIS WRATH.
It is a prophecy that is so singular in description and so universal in its impact that it cannot be overlooked by any serious student of the Word of God. Although we know that God is involved to some degree in the entire unfolding of events associated with the 7 seals, it is the breaking of the 6th seal that plunges the world into direct confrontation with God almighty. The heaven shakes mightily, the earth shakes violently, stuff falls from the atmosphere, the light from the sun and moon is considerably diminished [presumably from the smoke, dust and debris in the atmosphere] and every person on the planet cowers before the Great Day of His Wrath!

This great day emphasizes the inevitability of God's move to re-take the planet for the Son. The unstoppable march began with the opening of the 1st seal, and now a divinely appointed moment displays to the entire universe that this is not just a man-made quarrelling of the nations, but a God-determined, God-implemented, God-appointed process for the reclamation of the planet from those who would destroy it.

And I beheld when he had opened the sixth seal, and, lo, there was a great earthquake; and the sun became black as sackcloth of hair, and the moon became as blood; And the stars of heaven fell unto the earth, even as a fig tree casteth her untimely figs, when she is shaken of a mighty wind. And the heaven departed as a scroll when it is rolled together; and every mountain and island were moved out of their places. And the kings of the earth, and the great men, and the rich men, and the chief captains, and the mighty men, and every bondman, and every free man, hid themselves in the dens and in the rocks of the mountains; And said to the mountains and rocks, Fall on us, and hide us from the face of him that sitteth on the throne, and from the wrath of the Lamb: For the great day of his wrath is come; and who shall be able to stand?
Revelation 6: 12-17

At this time there is only one seal left to break. This final 7th seal contains within it, 7 trumpet judgments and 7 bowl judgments. It is the unleashing of God's fury upon a world that has thoroughly scorned his forgiveness and grace. A world that has mocked his humble approach of love; a world that has oppressed, tortured, and killed many of his faithful followers; a world that is entrenched in its love of darkness; a world that hates holiness, and loves unrighteousness. Chapter 7 gives us a glimpse of the multitude of saints in heaven who have faithfully endured during two thousand years of Great Tribulation (not seven) while patiently praying: Thy kingdom come, thy will be done on earth as it is in heaven.

Finally, The Great Day of His Wrath has come. Although another 3 ½ years remain before it is completed, His wrath has begun and nothing will stop it until both the final mortal and immortal enemies are overthrown!

And when he had opened the seventh seal, there was silence in heaven about the space of half an hour. And I saw the seven angels which stood before God; and to them were given seven trumpets. And another angel came and stood at the altar, having a golden censer; and there was given unto him much incense, that he should offer it with the prayers of all saints upon the golden altar which was before the throne. And the smoke of the incense, which came with the prayers of the saints, ascended up before God out of the angel's hand. And the angel took the censer, and filled it with fire of the altar, and cast it into the earth: and there were voices, and thunderings, and lightnings, and an earthquake.
Revelation 8:1-5

The amazing reality is that throughout the final 3 ½ years before Christ returns to the earth; the temple in heaven remains open to the repentant heart. Even in this final hour of wrath, God keeps the door open for the person wanting to reconcile with Him. Oh, the wonderful, matchless grace of God! Not until the 3 ½ years are expired does God finally close off the temple from those who might wish to repent. It's simply too late!

And after that I looked, and, behold, the temple of the tabernacle of the testimony in heaven was opened: And the seven angels came out of the temple, having the seven plagues, clothed in pure and white linen, and having their breasts girded with golden girdles. And one of the four beasts gave unto the seven angels seven golden vials full of the wrath of God, who liveth for ever and ever. And the temple was filled with smoke from the glory of God, and from his power; and no man was able to enter into the temple, till the seven plagues of the seven angels were fulfilled. <u>Revelation 15:5-8</u>

What matchless glory awaits those who are over comers in this world. By the same token, what misery awaits those who scorn His mercy, and despise His grace. For these unfortunate souls, the worst of Satan's malice, the worst of man's fallen nature, and the worst of the wrath of an angry God is all that is left to endure, until all the kingdoms of this world fall and Christ returns to reign eternally with his saints!

The Coming Paradigm Shift

The world may not know it yet; the saints of God may not readily understand it yet; but a great paradigm shift is coming very soon.
If you look up the word "paradigm" in Webster's Collegiate Dictionary, you will find a very short description for the meaning. It says, to show side by side.   Then as synonyms it adds the words "example" and "pattern". This discussion about the coming paradigm shift will make use of the word, "pattern".   We will also look primarily at the "biblical" description of the coming shift in pattern.   Biblical paradigm shifts are not unusual, but they are rare occasions.

There are various opinions about these shifts and what they may mean to us who consider ourselves to be believers of the bible. Here, are seven of them that readily appear to my mind.

1.   When Adam & Eve were put out of the Garden of Eden
2.   When the entire earth was flooded
3.   When Nimrod rose to power and began the tower of Babel
4.   When the earth split apart in the days of Peleg
5.   When God called Abram
6.   When God called Moses
7.   When Christ Jesus came to Earth

When Adam & Eve left the Garden of Eden, the rules changed, and their entire way of life, including their relationship with God, changed drastically.   Do you recall God saying:

" Unto the woman he said, I will greatly multiply thy sorrow and thy conception; in sorrow thou shalt bring forth children; and thy desire shall be to thy husband, and he shall rule over thee.   And unto Adam he said, Because thou hast hearkened unto the voice of thy wife, and hast eaten of the tree, of which I commanded thee, saying, Thou shalt not eat of it: cursed is the ground for thy sake; in sorrow shalt thou eat of it all the days of thy life;   Thorns also and thistles shall it bring forth to thee; and thou shalt eat the herb of the field;   In the sweat of thy face shalt thou eat bread, till thou return

unto the ground; for out of it wast thou taken: for dust thou art, and unto dust shalt thou return." Genesis 3:16-19

Here is a good example of the paradigm or pattern shifting in their lives. You can see the two patterns side by side. First the way things were in the garden, and then the way things were outside the garden. Centuries later when the flood occurred, once again there was a paradigm shift. The relationship between man and animals changed. Meat became a standard part of the human diet as well as herbs. Rules about blood were set up, and a law concerning murder was instituted.

And the fear of you and the dread of you shall be upon every beast of the earth, and upon every fowl of the air, upon all that moveth upon the earth, and upon all the fishes of the sea; into your hand are they delivered. Every moving thing that liveth shall be meat for you; even as the green herb have I given you all things. But flesh with the life thereof, which is the blood thereof, shall ye not eat. And surely your blood of your lives will I require; at the hand of every beast will I require it, and at the hand of man; at the hand of every man's brother will I require the life of man. Whoso sheddeth man's blood, by man shall his blood be shed: for in the image of God made he man. Genesis 9:2-6

Another paradigm shift happened in the days of Nimrod. Among other things, the worship of God was drastically changed; a tyrannical ruler began enforcing his will upon others; the unity of government was shattered; and men's languages changed resulting in the division into races of people on the earth.

And the LORD came down to see the city and the tower, which the children of men builded. And the LORD said, Behold, the people is one, and they have all one language; and this they begin to do: and now nothing will be restrained from them, which they have imagined to do. Go to, let us go down, and there confound their language, that they may not understand one another's speech. So the LORD scattered them abroad from thence upon the face of all the earth: Genesis 11:5-8

45

Even the events of Peleg's day made some shifts in the pattern of things. We're not given the details, but the event that took place 101years after the flood, was so dynamic that it resulted in some major physical changes to the planet, and surely left a mark on the people who came through the experience. Who knows all the ramifications that resulted from the very earth dividing up, in a way that was completely different than the old paradigm. It may be that this was the time that Native Americans were first separated as a people from others on the planet, and the Aborigines of Australia were cut off from other civilizations.

And unto Eber were born two sons: the name of one was Peleg; for in his days was the earth divided; and his brother's name was Joktan. Genesis 10:25

As great the impact may have been upon the human race in Peleg's day, it cannot be any less dramatic, than when God, himself entered the cosmos to call out Abram to separate him to Himself. As we know from scripture he became the Father of many nations. As we know from history, his offspring came to espouse the three major mono-theistic religions of the world, Judaism, Christianity, and Islam. This paradigm shift absolutely transformed the rest of history to be written about this earth! As Christians, we know that through Abraham came Christ, our savior, into this world. What a great impact this shift made compared to the paradigms that came before it.

Now the LORD had said unto Abram, Get thee out of thy country, and from thy kindred, and from thy father's house, unto a land that I will shew thee: And I will make of thee a great nation, and I will bless thee, and make thy name great; and thou shalt be a blessing: And I will bless them that bless thee, and curse him that curseth thee: and in thee shall all families of the earth be blessed. Genesis12:1-3

Centuries later, we see God intervening into the affairs of men by calling a man named Moses into His service. Through this single man, God made a covenant with a select group of people that has impacted the world down to this very day. This paradigm shift brought a spiritual, and eternal shift into the direction and purpose of human beings on this earth.

"Therefore, come now, and I will send you to Pharaoh, so that you may bring My people, the sons of Israel, out of Egypt." But Moses said to God, "Who am I, that I should go to Pharaoh, and that I should bring the sons of Israel out of Egypt?" And He said, "Certainly I will be with you, and this shall be the sign to you that it is I who have sent you: when you have brought the people out of Egypt, you shall worship God at this mountain."
Exodus 3:10-12

Now therefore, if ye will obey my voice indeed, and keep my covenant, then ye shall be a peculiar treasure unto me above all people: for all the earth is mine: And ye shall be unto me a kingdom of priests, and an holy nation. These are the words which thou shalt speak unto the children of Israel. And Moses came and called for the elders of the people, and laid before their faces all these words which the LORD commanded him. And all the people answered together, and said, All that the LORD hath spoken we will do. Exodus 19:5-8

And finally, we come to the greatest paradigm shift of all the previous ages. It happened when Jesus of Nazareth, the Son of the Living God, emptied himself and became a baby born of a woman.

Let this mind be in you, which was also in Christ Jesus: Who, being in the form of God, thought it not robbery to be equal with God: But made himself of no reputation, and took upon him the form of a servant, and was made in the likeness of men: And being found in fashion as a man, he humbled himself, and became obedient unto death, even the death of the cross. Wherefore God also hath highly exalted him, and given him a name which is above every name: That at the name of Jesus every knee should bow, of things in heaven, and things in earth, and things under the earth; Philippians 2:5-10

It was this paradigm shift that has most affected this world. When you lay the two paradigms side by side [Moses' and Jesus'], you instantly see changes in the new pattern that Jesus instituted.

Ye have heard that it was said by them of old time, Thou shalt not kill; and whosoever shall kill shall be in danger of the judgment: But I say unto you, That whosoever is angry with his brother without a cause shall be in danger of the judgment: Matthew 5:21:22

Over and over Jesus repeated this phrase, "Ye have heard it said…But I say unto you". Although, Jesus fulfilled every part of the Old Covenant, he set about to establish an even better covenant. This should have come as no surprise, because Moses and other prophets were told of His coming, and the paradigm shift they could expect.

The LORD thy God will raise up unto thee a Prophet from the midst of thee, of thy brethren, like unto me; unto him ye shall hearken;... I will raise them up a Prophet from among their brethren, like unto thee, and will put my words in his mouth; and he shall speak unto them all that I shall command him. And it shall come to pass, that whosoever will not hearken unto my words which he shall speak in my name, I will require it of him. Deuteronomy 18:15-19

Behold, the days come, saith the LORD, that I will make a new covenant with the house of Israel, and with the house of Judah: Not according to the covenant that I made with their fathers in the day that I took them by the hand to bring them out of the land of Egypt; which my covenant they brake, although I was an husband unto them, saith the LORD: But this shall be the covenant that I will make with the house of Israel; After those days, saith the LORD, I will put my law in their inward parts, and write it in their hearts; and will be their God, and they shall be my people. Jeremiah 31:31-33

In spite of the fact that God foretold of the coming of Jesus, it was still very difficult for people to make the jump from one paradigm to the other. As with all of us, a paradigm shift is a most difficult

48

thing for us to assess, and then to align ourselves with. When some of the people around Jesus were pointing out some of the obvious differences in the pattern or paradigm Jesus was introducing compared to Moses', He said these words:

...No man putteth a piece of a new garment upon an old; if otherwise, then both the new maketh a rent, and the piece that was taken out of the new agreeth not with the old. And no man putteth new wine into old bottles; else the new wine will burst the bottles, and be spilled, and the bottles shall perish. But new wine must be put into new bottles; and both are preserved. No man also having drunk old wine straightway desireth new: for he saith, The old is better Luke 5:36-39

The old orthodoxy is always easier to hold on to, and feels much more secure than a new one suddenly introduced and untested. Little wonder that most Jews rejected Christ.

In the same way people of every age are reluctant or hesitant to leave one paradigm and leap into another; and so will many of God's people be stunned and hesitant to move with the Spirit of God in the upcoming paradigm shift. A shift is coming, and it will take place whether we Christians are ready or not. Jesus emphasized it over and over through the gospels, and through the book of Revelation, that we need to prepare for this coming shift. The sad news is that many will not be prepared for the impending paradigm shift at all. The following phrase is repeated in Revelation seven times; yet, even this is not enough to cause men to prepare for the events ahead.

He that hath an ear, let him hear what the Spirit saith unto the churches;" Revelation 2 & 3

A lot of believers foresee only one paradigm shift coming in the years ahead. They see the one established when Jesus comes again to set up his millennial reign on earth. The truth is there is one more paradigm shift that will take place 3 ½ years before Christ comes to establish His Kingdom on earth. Although it is only a 3 ½ year paradigm, it will affect the inhabitants of the world more drastically than all the previous shifts on earth.

And take heed to yourselves, lest at any time your hearts be overcharged with surfeiting, and drunkenness, and cares of this life, and so that day come upon you unawares. For as a snare shall it come on all them that dwell on the face of the whole earth. Watch ye therefore, and pray always, that ye may be accounted worthy to escape all these things that shall come to pass, and to stand before the Son of man. Luke 21:34-36

For the most part, Christians seem content to rest upon their "salvation" as evidence of their own preparedness for this coming shift. Several things however, belie their misplaced confidence. For one thing, Jesus was addressing Christians when he warned them to watch and pray that they might be counted worthy to escape what was coming upon the whole earth. If in fact "salvation" was sufficient grounds for escaping, why then would Jesus urge them to take steps to be worthy. The very word worthy indicates achievement of something deserved or merited. If "salvation" is all that is needed at the time of this huge shift in the paradigm, then why the repeated, seven-fold injunction to hear what the Spirit says to the churches in the book of Revelation? Many a saint is approaching the coming day unaware, and unconcerned about the preparations needed to make the leap from the existing paradigm into the next one revealed by scripture. Perhaps some are lazy in heart, or dull of hearing. Perhaps too some are relying upon their denominational founders and leaders rather than actively seeking to know, "what the Spirit is saying?"

In a parable about the believers at the end of the age, Jesus divided believers into two distinct categories. It would appear that every believer will be found in one or the other category when Jesus returns. Here's what he likened the Kingdom of God to be at the time of the end. Take note that he is describing the kingdom, the Church, if you will. Not those who are outside of the family of faith.

Then shall the kingdom of heaven be likened unto ten virgins, which took their lamps, and went forth to meet the bridegroom.   And five of them were wise, and five were foolish.   Matthew 25:1-2

Please note that they were all anticipating the coming of the bridegroom, [all were believers, not unbelievers] but some were wise, and the others were foolish.   The sad part in this description by Jesus is that each virgin [Christian] held their destiny in their own hands,   and could have been prepared for the moment, thereby avoiding the starkest paradigm shift the inhabitants of earth will ever experience up to that time.   The only difference between the waiting virgins… Some had oil because they were wise; and some had no oil because they were foolish!

They that were foolish took their lamps, and took no oil with them: But the wise took oil in their vessels with their lamps.
Matthew 25:3-4

And so, the inevitable happened!

And at midnight there was a cry made, Behold, the bridegroom cometh; go ye out to meet him.   Then all those virgins arose, and trimmed their lamps.   And the foolish said unto the wise, Give us of your oil; for our lamps are gone out.   But the wise answered, saying, Not so; lest there be not enough for us and you: but go ye rather to them that sell, and buy for yourselves.   And while they went to buy, the bridegroom came; and they that were ready went in with him to the marriage, and the door was shut.
Matthew 25:6-11

What a bleak statement and, what a pitiful result!
"The door was shut"

Afterward came also the other virgins, saying, Lord, Lord, open to us.   But he answered and said, Verily I say unto you, I know you not.   Watch therefore, for ye know neither the day nor the hour wherein the Son of man cometh.   Matthew 25:11-13

I can't think of a plainer way the Lord could have shown his disciples that a separation would be made among his followers. The moment of this separation is well documented by a host of scriptures which we will look at soon. The important thing to gather from this parable is to notice that a division is coming to the people of God. It will come at the moment of the next great paradigm shift. It will determine which paradigm every living believer will be thrust into. One paradigm will be absolutely glorious! The other one will be absolutely hellacious! Among the New Testament verses verifying this coming separation are the following:

And unto the angel of the church of the Laodiceans write; These things saith the Amen, the faithful and true witness, the beginning of the creation of God; I know thy works, that thou art neither cold nor hot: I would thou wert cold or hot. So then because thou art lukewarm, and neither cold nor hot, I will spue thee out of my mouth. <u>Revelation 3:14-17</u>

Here is a direct reference to this event from Jesus' own mouth as he addresses the believers living at the close of the Church age, represented by the Laodicean Church. These were not wicked, vile people. These were people who had run out of oil and had no way of holding the light of God within their hearts and minds. When the next paradigm shift takes place in this world, these poor, blind saints will be spewed out as something distasteful and nauseating. The paradigm that they will be thrust into is clearly shown in the book of Revelation. We will look at those scriptures for a better grasp of what awaits those believers who are foolish and unprepared at the time of this event. On the other hand, the wise enter into a place where further access is then closed off. They too enter into a very different paradigm shift that the scriptures reveal in the book of Revelation. We'll look at that too in a minute. For now, let's look at some other places that describe this coming separation within the church of the Lord, Jesus Christ!

The lord of that servant shall come in a day when he looketh not for him, and in an hour that he is not aware of, And shall cut him asunder, and appoint him his portion with the hypocrites: there shall be weeping and gnashing of teeth. Matthew 24:50-51

Here Christ is speaking of his own servants. These are servants who are not prepared for His coming and are cut apart from those who are ready and prepared for his return. Instead they must endure the portion of those who are mere hypocrites. There will certainly be a lot of regret, but no way of changing the discipline ahead.

But of that day and hour knoweth no man, no, not the angels of heaven, but my Father only. But as the days of Noe were, so shall also the coming of the Son of man be. For as in the days that were before the flood they were eating and drinking, marrying and giving in marriage, until the day that Noe entered into the ark, And knew not until the flood came, and took them all away; so shall also the coming of the Son of man be. Then shall two be in the field; the one shall be taken, and the other left. Two women shall be grinding at the mill; the one shall be taken, and the other left. Watch therefore: for ye know not what hour your Lord doth come. But know this, that if the goodman of the house had known in what watch the thief would come, he would have watched, and would not have suffered his house to be broken up. Therefore be ye also ready: for in such an hour as ye think not the Son of man cometh.
Matthew 24:37-42

Some may want to apply this portion of scripture to those who are lost and outside of the household of faith. However, the admonitions are to his own followers, not to "outsiders". It is the believer that has to be watching or lose an opportunity. Jesus never instructs non-believers to watch and pray. To add to this evidence of a coming paradigm shift, let's read what is said about the church in Revelation Chapter 12. Here again, we will see a separation taking place within the very household of faith!

And there appeared a great wonder in heaven; a woman clothed with the sun, and the moon under her feet, and upon her head a crown of twelve stars: And she being with child cried, travailing in birth, and pained to be delivered. And there appeared another wonder in heaven; and behold a great red dragon, having seven heads and ten horns, and seven crowns upon his heads. And his tail drew the third part of the stars of heaven, and did cast them to the earth: and the dragon stood before the woman which was ready to be delivered, for to devour her child as soon as it was born. And she brought forth a man child, who was to rule all nations with a rod of iron: and her child was caught up unto God, and to his throne. And the woman fled into the wilderness, where she hath a place prepared of God, that they should feed her there a thousand two hundred and threescore days.   Revelation 12:1-5

Take a close look at this descriptive passage and notice these things. In spite of all the imagery and metaphor, anyone should readily see that the woman is cared for by God, and that from that woman, a strong, manly child is first separated and then caught up to the throne of God to begin ruling and reigning with Him.

With this in mind, let us move on to see more closely, the detail which God has given us concerning these tremendous events of the future.   Let the reader determine for him or herself the truth of the next idea presented, but adequate study will show that the woman signifies, quite accurately, the Church in all her glory and authority. She's clothed with the sun even as the Church is clothed with light…*Ye are the light of the world. A city that is set on an hill cannot be hid.* Matthew 5:14

She is crowned with 12 stars [Apostles] and she has the moon [ruler of darkness] under her feet where Jesus placed her.

Then he called his twelve disciples together, and gave them power and authority over all devils Luke 9:1

Behold, I give unto you power to tread on serpents and scorpions, and over all the power of the enemy: and nothing shall by any means hurt you. Luke 10:19

But most intriguing of all, this woman is travailing in pain with child. The symbolic picture continues to unfold like a movie. The woman gives birth to a manchild that is caught up to the very throne of God and the woman retreats into the wilderness for a very specific time period of three and one half years, while being hounded by satan.

Here we have once again an unmistakable account of a coming separation within the very church of the Lord Jesus Christ. Earlier we reviewed Christ's own account of his determination to spew a portion of his church out of his mouth. We heard his account of ten virgins divided into two groups with one entering in and the door being shut. We heard his account of the two in the field and two grinding when one was taken and the other left. And now we have this account given us in Revelation Chapter 12 of the church going through a separation with the child being caught up to heaven and the woman fleeing into the wilderness for three and one half years before the final harvest depicted in Chapter 14.

For many, this is a disturbing idea. If it disturbs you, count yourself among the blessed. It is those described by Jesus in Revelation 3 that will not be disturbed by this knowledge.

So then because thou art lukewarm, and neither cold nor hot, I will spue thee out of my mouth. Because thou sayest, I am rich, and increased with goods, and have need of nothing; and knowest not that thou art wretched, and miserable, and poor, and blind, and naked: Revelation 3:16-17

The group of Saints undisturbed by this report are of this class. They don't know, and they are blind. And in the estimation of the savior, they are wretched, miserable, poor, and blind and naked! He loves them.... But they refuse to be wise and learn the easy way. Instead they will be required to learn the hard way of discipline. Unlike the saints just preceding the final laodicean church age. Of whom Jesus said:

Because thou hast kept the word of my patience, I also will keep thee from the hour of temptation, [discipline] which shall come upon all the world, to try [prove and test] them that dwell upon the earth. Revelation 3:10

If you find yourself disturbed by the Master's words, then give heed to what he requires.

I counsel thee to buy of me gold tried in the fire, that thou mayest be rich; and white raiment, that thou mayest be clothed, and that the shame of thy nakedness do not appear; and anoint thine eyes with eyesalve, that thou mayest see. Revelation 3:18

Do everything within your power to discover what this means and DO IT!

*And why call ye me, Lord, Lord, and do not the things which I say? Whosoever cometh to me, and **heareth my sayings, and doeth them**, I will shew you to whom he is like: He is like a man which built an house, and digged deep, and laid the foundation on a rock: and when the flood arose, the stream beat vehemently upon that house, and could not shake it: for it was founded upon a rock. **But he that heareth, and doeth not**, is like a man that without a foundation built an house upon the earth; against which the stream did beat vehemently, and immediately it fell; and the ruin of that house was great.* Luke 6:46-49

Now that we've seen from several sources in the scripture that a paradigm shift is coming upon this world.   Let's take a closer look at what the two paradigms will look like for the believers in Christ. Let's begin with the group made up of wise virgins.   What exactly is the paradigm going to look like, that they enter into?   We have ample scripture given to us that we might comprehend the parameters of this most unusual paradigm shift; for those who have oil burning, who are watching and praying, and who are looking for the bridegroom to come. So, let's inspect them one by one and pray that God will enable us to see what he, the Spirit, is saying to the churches!

First of all, we know already that they are caught up to the throne of God. They actually begin a very special union with the Father upon His very throne.

To him that overcometh will I grant to sit with me in my throne, even as I also overcame, and am set down with my Father in his throne.
Revelation 3:21

Although this should not surprise us as believers, it's still hard to comprehend that God could or would want us to share in such a hallowed position of authority. We are all very well aware of our short-comings, our weaknesses, our failures, our sin. It seems incomprehensible that God would plan to bring mankind into this kind of relationship; and yet the scripture is full of a host of verifying verses declaring this very paradigm for the overcoming saint! To begin with, look at God's stated intention for the human race as mentioned in the book of Hebrews:

For it was fitting that he, for whom and by whom all things exist, in bringing many sons to glory, should make the founder of their salvation perfect through suffering.
Hebrews 2:10 [English Standard Version]

It's clear from this passage that God's eternal plan was a mission of bringing many sons into a glorified state, just as he himself enjoys. His completed plan of redemption involves changing our soul, our spirit, and our body. Our spirit is regenerated at the moment we are born again, or born of the Spirit. At that moment we have God's nature within us. That's why John could write and say:
Whosoever is born of God doth not commit sin; for his seed remaineth in him: and he cannot sin, because he is born of God.
I John 3:9

Naturally, we all sin and fall short, but it is not something that springs from the nature of God in us. The spirit born of God cannot sin. All sin springs from the "old man" or the old nature in us, which needs to be put off, Paul said. Although, we are born of the Spirit instantaneously, our soul is slowly changed in character, over time.   It is formed in us through a multitude of difficult choices we make following Christ.

And we all, with unveiled face, beholding the glory of the Lord, being transformed into the same image from one degree of glory to another;   For this comes from the Lord who is the Spirit.
II Corinthians 3:18   [English Standard Version]

This process of changing the very character of our soul is life- long.   It's tedious at times and very difficult.   It requires absolute discipleship to Christ, a denying of ourselves and a taking up of our cross and following Him.   It involves pain, and suffering.   It requires an intake of His word, being transformed by renewing our minds, and a deepening love for Him, if the soul is to be changed like His.   *…the accuser of our brethren is cast down, which accused them before our God day and night.   And they overcame him by the blood of the Lamb, and by the word of their testimony; and they loved not their lives unto the death.*   Revelation 12:10-11

However, when the process is finally completed, a disciple stands made in the image of His master, Jesus!

The disciple is not above his master: but every one that is perfect shall be as his master.   Luke 6:40

This process we speak of will not be completed until we actually "see" Him.   At that moment we will be made perfect.

Beloved now are we the sons of God, and it doth not yet appear what we shall be: but we know that, when he shall appear, we shall be like him; for we shall see him as he is.   And every man that hath this hope in him purifieth himself, even as he is pure.   I John 3:2-3

We'd all like to "arrive" at perfection.   The truth is we are perfected only after death.

To the general assembly and church of the firstborn, which are written in heaven, and to God the Judge of all, and to <u>*the spirits of just men made perfect,*</u> Hebrews 12:23

There is at least one exception to this rule and that is shown to us in the Book of Revelation. It is in this book that God shows us a special group of people who will experience this change while they are still alive. This third change; [the change of our body into a glorified body] also happens instantaneously just as our spirit was regenerated instantaneously by the Spirit of God. Paul describes it like this:

Behold, I shew you a mystery; We shall not all sleep, but we shall all be changed, In a moment, in the twinkling of an eye, at the last trump: for the trumpet shall sound, and the dead shall be raised incorruptible, and we shall be changed. For this corruptible must put on incorruption, and this mortal must put on immortality. I Corinthians 15:51-53

There are definitely some wonderful changes ahead for the believer at the sound of the last trumpet. However, there is one other occasion when some believers will experience this change of the body. It will take place 3 ½ years before the final trumpet of Revelation. Few Christians are aware of this special and unique moment when some of Christ's followers will receive this "perfection" and be glorified on the spot while they are still alive in their mortal bodies! We're all so familiar with Paul's writings where he shares the revelation given to him about our future change in the twinkling of an eye. We are well rehearsed about the dead rising first then we which are alive and remain being changed into a glorified state. But few have searched the book of Revelation to see that Christ has unveiled a mystery not shown to Paul. Paul was given a glimpse of the events at the final trump when the harvest of God's people takes place. The harvest Jesus himself spoke about when he was here on earth.

And then shall appear the sign of the Son of man in heaven: and then shall all the tribes of the earth mourn, and they shall see the Son of man coming in the clouds of heaven with power and great glory. And he shall send his angels with a great sound of a trumpet, and they shall gather together his elect from the four winds, from one end of heaven to the other. <u>Matthew 24:30-31</u>

Let both grow together until the harvest: and in the time of harvest I will say to the reapers, Gather ye together first the tares, and bind them in bundles to burn them: but gather the wheat into my barn. <u>Matthew 13:30</u> [See the Chart Chapter 17]

As therefore the tares are gathered and burned in the fire; so shall it be in the end of this world. The Son of man shall send forth his angels, and they shall gather out of his kingdom all things that offend, and them which do iniquity; <u>Matthew 13:40-41</u>

In the book of Revelation, Jesus gives us some further insight into matters revolving around the end of the age. One of those things relates directly to the paradigm shift we have been tracing in His Word. We have seen that the followers of Christ will experience a time of separation at the close of the age. If you recall, we read scriptures that denoted a group of people designated as "wise virgins" , "the manchild", "the one taken", "the ones not spewed out of Christ's mouth". These all speak metaphorically of a group of believers who are ripe, mature, and ready at the end of the age. These all describe a group of believers that are counted worthy to escape what is coming upon the whole world for a period of 3 ½ years at the end of the age.   These people are not part of the general harvest spoken of by Paul and Jesus.   These people make up a company referred to in Revelation as the First Fruits unto God and the Lamb. Just as any natural crop has the first ripe and mature fruit followed by the general harvest, so God has revealed that He too will have a first fruits company followed by the general harvest of all believers both from heaven and earth! [Deceased or living]
These are they which were not defiled with women; for they are virgins. These are they which follow the Lamb whithersoever he goeth. These were redeemed from among men, being the firstfruits unto God and to the Lamb. <u>Revelation 14:4</u>

Let's take a closer look at the scriptures that speak of this very unique company of people who are "glorified" 3 ½ years before the general harvest at the coming of Christ. Keeping in mind God's purpose for mankind, let us see what he proclaims about the process of bringing many sons into Glory with himself [a glorified state of being] . One of the first things we notice about this company of people is that they are alive on the planet at the time of their glorification. They are not deceased saints, and they are on the earth at the time of the end. In fact two times the scriptures make it clear that these are living people on the earth. Both times, the scriptures indicate that they are "redeemed" from among men, or from the earth!

And they sung as it were a new song before the throne, and before the four beasts, and the elders: and no man could learn that song but the hundred and forty and four thousand, which were redeemed from the earth. These are they which were not defiled with women; for they are virgins. These are they which follow the Lamb whithersoever he goeth. These were redeemed from among men, being the firstfruits unto God and to the Lamb. Revelation 14:3-4

This company of believers is fully redeemed. Many of us refer to the entire process of our salvation as being "redeemed". And, in truth, we are redeemed because Christ paid for our redemption. But, the process is not complete yet. We're all being changed from glory to glory, but we have not yet been glorified with a new eternal body. Paul wrote of this occasion frequently, and asserted that our redemption would be complete at the moment we received our glorified bodies.

And not only they, but ourselves also, which have the firstfruits of the Spirit, even we ourselves groan within ourselves, waiting for the adoption, to wit, the redemption of our body. Romans 8:23

...ye were sealed with that holy Spirit of promise, Which is the earnest of our inheritance until the redemption of the purchased possession, unto the praise of his glory. Ephesians 1:13-14

Even Jesus made it clear that our completed redemption was something that would take place in the future at the time of the end.

And then shall they see the Son of man coming in a cloud with power and great glory. And when these things begin to come to pass, then look up, and lift up your heads; for your redemption draweth nigh. Luke 21:27-28

Now, returning to the book of Revelation to pick up once again what it tells us about this company of believers who are separated from the rest of believers and transported into an entirely different paradigm and labeled "The First Fruits unto God and The Lamb", let us see what else God reveals to us.

And after these things I saw four angels standing on the four corners of the earth, holding the four winds of the earth, that the wind should not blow on the earth, nor on the sea, nor on any tree. And I saw another angel ascending from the east, having the seal of the living God: and he cried with a loud voice to the four angels, to whom it was given to hurt the earth and the sea, Saying, Hurt not the earth, neither the sea, nor the trees, till we have sealed the servants of our God in their foreheads. Revelation 7:1-3

Here we see a most unusual event transpire. God is about to pour out his wrath upon a wicked and rebellious human race. [see chart] But, before a single trumpet is blown, and before any of his wrath touches a single thing on earth, He first "seals" his servants in the forehead. These are the wise virgins, this is the manchild company, these are the first fruits unto God and the Lamb. These are the "hot" saints, not the "lukewarm" saints. This special "sealing" is described as being done to the forehead. Like a Sunkist orange, this fruit is proclaimed ready by God and is forthwith sealed in the forehead, or mind. This is God bringing the disciple to perfection. This is the work of God completing the discipleship process. It is my considered opinion, that the people receiving this seal in their forehead will never entertain another contrary thought to the Will of God again. We currently struggle daily with thoughts contrary to the Will of God. I am persuaded that at that moment, this company of people will never wrestle with another contrary thought to the perfect Will of God. It appears they are no longer subject to the temptations of the flesh, for they have glorified bodies. Satan no longer tempts them and the lusts of this world have no more power over them. In fact, another verse describing them indicates they have actually received the very Character of God in their minds. They have his very name written in there!

And I looked, and, lo, a Lamb stood on the mount Sion, and with him an hundred forty and four thousand, having his Father's name written in their foreheads. Revelation 14:1

This fourteenth chapter of Revelation contains a detailed description of this company of believers. We find out amazing details about the new paradigm they have entered.

And I heard a voice from heaven, as the voice of many waters, and as the voice of a great thunder: and I heard the voice of harpers harping with their harps: And they sung as it were a new song before the throne, and before the four beasts, and the elders: and no man could learn that song but the hundred and forty and four thousand, which were redeemed from the earth. These are they which were not defiled with women; for they are virgins. These are they which follow the Lamb whithersoever he goeth. These were redeemed from among men, being the firstfruits unto God and to the Lamb. And in their mouth was found no guile: for they are without fault before the throne of God. Revelation 14:2-5

This special company is special indeed! They are victorious overcomers and therefore have the accompanying harps. They sing a song only they have the right to sing. Throughout scripture, you find people inventing songs when they have had a special experience with God. David did it. Miriam [sister of Moses] did it. And here we see this company bursting into song expressing the experience they and they alone, are having with God as the very first group of people to experience this new paradigm! They are redeemed from the earth and will forever enjoy the delights of a glorified body like their master Jesus has enjoyed since rising from His own grave. They are pure virgins undefiled with women. Simply put, they are totally espoused to Christ and have had no communion with any other form of idolatry or spiritual fornication. In fact, in their mouths is no guile, deceit, or lies…only the Truth! There total devotion is to the Lamb, their redeemer, and they follow Him wherever He leads them. They are the FIRSTFRUITS UNTO GOD AND THE LAMB! They "stand" before the very throne of God almighty, indicating that they will be involved in the execution of God's will from the throne! The great harvest is yet to be gathered, but here, wise and prepared, stands the first fruits of God's eternal plan of bringing many sons into Glory! Here stands a company of believers that fully match up to the number representative of, and assigned to their company. Their number is 144,000. They are not only part of a ruling party as enumerated by the number 12. They not only represent the redemption of the Israel of God made up of a full 12 tribes…

For in Christ Jesus neither circumcision availeth any thing, nor uncircumcision, but a new creature. And as many as walk according to this rule, peace be on them, and mercy, and upon the Israel of God. Galatians 6:15-16

Not as though the word of God hath taken none effect. For they are not all Israel, which are of Israel: Neither, because they are the seed of Abraham, are they all children: but, In Isaac shall thy seed be called. That is, They which are the children of the flesh, these are not the children of God: but the children of the promise are counted for the seed. Romans 9:6-8

…They also represent a group of human disciples elevated to the realm of the Spirit of God indicated by the multiplication of 1000. This group represents the power and wisdom and victory of God almighty when He purposed within himself to bring many sons into Glory. This special group, just like the first fruits offered to God in the O.T. display to one and all that God's manifold wisdom will prevail against all odds, and points to the coming harvest when God will gather his elect from the four winds [those living on earth] and from one end of heaven to the other [the dead in Christ] at the sound of the last trump of God!   Should not the heart of every believer be stirred to press for this glorious high calling of God?

Brethren, I count not myself to have apprehended: but this one thing I do, forgetting those things which are behind, and reaching forth unto those things which are before, I press toward the mark for the prize of the high calling of God in Christ Jesus.
Philippians 3:13-14

What we have just pondered, is a description of the monumental paradigm shift coming to a select group of saints living at the end of the age; the number 144,000 reflecting in piercing accuracy their station in eternal glory.   Just as God used 7 churches to depict the entirety of the "church age", so here he uses a number that reflects the completeness, the fullness, the utter ascendancy of this victorious, princely Israel of God.   Some take it to mean physical, national Israel, but the fact that the tribe of Dan and the tribe of Ephraim are not listed is another indication that this is not a realistic list of the natural Israel, but a symbolic picture of the firstfruits unto God and the Lamb.   When this group enters the coming paradigm shift, the words of Jesus will suddenly take on greater fulfillment and life.

If ye abide in me, and my words abide in you, ye shall ask what ye will, and it shall be done unto you.   Herein is my Father glorified, that ye bear much fruit; so shall ye be my disciples. John 15:7-8

Verily, verily, I say unto you, He that believeth on me, the works that I do shall he do also; and greater works than these shall he do; because I go unto my Father.   And whatsoever ye shall ask in my name, that will I do, that the Father may be glorified in the Son.   If ye shall ask any thing in my name, I will do it.
John 14:12-14

Jesus said unto her, I am the resurrection, and the life: he that believeth in me, though he were dead, yet shall he live: And whosoever liveth and believeth in me shall never die. Believest thou this?   John 11:25-26

Your fathers did eat manna in the wilderness, and are dead.   This is the bread which cometh down from heaven, that a man may eat thereof and not die.   John 6:49-50

This body of believers will never taste death!   This body of believers will be exactly as their master, who held absolute authority over disease, death, demons, and the elements.   Nothing was impossible to Christ, nor will it be for these "super saints" who are sealed in their foreheads and caught up to the throne.   We actually see them active on the earth to a certain degree during the 3 ½ years in which the earth is plunged into such awful holocaust.

And there came out of the smoke locusts upon the earth: and unto them was given power, as the scorpions of the earth have power. And it was commanded them that they should not hurt the grass of the earth, neither any green thing, neither any tree; but only those men which have not the seal of God in their foreheads. Revelation 8:3-4

And she brought forth a man child, who was to rule all nations with a rod of iron: and her child was caught up unto God, and to his throne.   And the woman fled into the wilderness, where she hath a place prepared of God, that they should feed her there a thousand two hundred and threescore days.   Revelation 12:5-6

There is no absolute proof that the ones feeding [nourishing] the woman [church] are the first fruits company [144,000]   but there's a strong suggestion that it is they themselves who care for the saints during this extremely hazardous time.   It is as if there is a whole host of "Jesuses" moving about in glorified bodies, caring for the portion of the church left behind.   These operate in the fullness of the Spirit just as Christ did while He was ministering on earth. Nothing shall be impossible to this company of believers in their glorified bodies.   Little wonder that the satanic creatures roaming about cannot harm these glorified saints!

The coming paradigm shift is not for everyone, even as it was not for everyone when Jesus came into the world. There were those who could not let go of their old orthodoxy to embrace the new and greater orthodoxy presented by the message of the Kingdom of God. Once again our world is heading straight into a new paradigm. For those who are earnestly seeking the Lord; for those who have heard his voice and opened the door; He is prepared to sit down and sup with them and enlighten them with the things that the Spirit saith unto the churches. Are you eagerly inviting Him in?

Behold, I stand at the door, and knock: if any man [in the church] hear my voice, and open the door, I will come in to him, and will sup with him, and he with me. To him that overcometh will I grant to sit with me in my throne, even as I also overcame, and am set down with my Father in his throne. He that hath an ear, let him hear what the Spirit saith unto the churches.·
Revelation 3:20-22

Now is the time for the saints of the most high God to make every effort to "follow the Lamb whithersoever He goeth!" Now is the time to earnestly watch and pray, making sure that we remain on guard against every effort of our enemy to derail our walk with God. Now is the time to stay in daily communion with God's Spirit. Now is the time to make sure we have ample oil in our lamps… or spirit energy in our soul, so that Christ will count us worthy to escape all that is coming upon this world and stand before Him in His glorious presence! Let us check our own hearts to see if there is any area of our life where our indifference has allowed Satan to lead us into self-centered thinking, self-centered speaking, or self-centered acting. Today is the day to turn around and begin following the Lamb wherever He leads. Today is the day to part with this world's way and begin taking up our cross with new fervor to follow Him. Today is the time to stop seeking our own life, and begin losing it for his sake. The moment of the new paradigm is drawing near. The book of Revelation shows us when that moment will unfold. Shall we proceed?

New Wine

We've just looked at the amazing paradigm shift that wise Christians will one day move into. It should spark in the child of God, a divine desire to live purely and walk closely with God.

but we know that, when he shall appear, we shall be like him; for we shall see him as he is. And every man that hath this hope in him purifieth himself, even as he is pure. I John 3:2-3

Watch ye therefore, and pray always, that ye may be accounted worthy to escape all these things that shall come to pass, and to stand before the Son of man. Luke 21:36

Sadly, there will be many who are too caught up with the cares of life, and the deceitfulness of riches to focus on this very important admonition. For these foolish Christians, and the rest of the unbelieving world, a brand new paradigm of unparalleled proportion awaits the commencement of God's pre-determined plan.

The paradigm described in Revelation and given to us by God is so unconventional that most Bible expositors cannot fathom the reality of what God plainly declares in this book. The majority of Christians want to cling to a well-formed, long-established orthodoxy. Orthodox doctrines offer foundation and stability to the one seeking after God. There's nothing more satisfying than to listen to or read from those who champion the orthodox teachings of the church. When I think of those who excel in apologetics, I can't help but think of men like Hank Hanegraaff. Men like him persuade us to anchor our souls to the solid teachings of scripture without wavering. Men and women in this kind of labor, bring us strength and surety in the tempest of life.

However, having said that, I must add that it is these very people who seem to struggle the most with understanding the book of Revelation. The book of Revelation is primarily a book that deals with the coming paradigm shift.   It can be most difficult to interpret its meanings while holding to the orthodoxy of the past.   For example, even the Apostle Paul struggled valiantly against the paradigm shift of his day.   He was well studied, very educated, extremely orthodox, and solidly entrenched in the paradigm of the Old Covenant.   His orthodoxy was so solid that it took a mighty persuasion for even God to get his attention and acceptance of a new paradigm.

there shined round about him a light from heaven: And he fell to the earth, and heard a voice saying unto him, Saul, Saul, why persecutest thou me?   And he said, Who art thou, Lord?   And the Lord said, I am Jesus whom thou persecutest: it is hard for thee to kick against the pricks.   Acts 9:3-5

Our heart goes out to Paul because he was trying to keep his feet on the old paradigm while God was moving him on to the next one.   The new one did not mean the old one was false; it merely meant that the old one was made void, and a new one with new parameters was now installed.   Anyone of us would have had a struggle too, changing from one paradigm to the next one on God's time table.   Look at the Apostle Peter.

Peter went up upon the housetop to pray about the sixth hour: And he became very hungry, and would have eaten: but while they made ready, he fell into a trance,   And saw heaven opened, and a certain vessel descending unto him, as it had been a great sheet knit at the four corners, and let down to the earth: Wherein were all manner of fourfooted beasts of the earth, and wild beasts, and creeping things, and fowls of the air.   And there came a voice to him, Rise, Peter; kill, and eat.   But Peter said, Not so, Lord; for I have never eaten any thing that is common or unclean.
Acts 10:9-14

God had to emphasize his purpose to change the paradigm again and again to Peter.   Even then Peter proceeded with great misgiving.   When he saw God unite with the Gentiles just as He had done with the Jews, Peter may have come close to passing out!   It simply

69

could not be this way in the old paradigm. It took all of this to convince Peter that God was changing the paradigm, and everything was "cool".

And he said unto them, Ye know how that it is an unlawful thing for a man that is a Jew to keep company, or come unto one of another nation; but God hath shewed me that I should not call any man common or unclean. Acts 10:28

Then Peter opened his mouth, and said, Of a truth I perceive that God is no respecter of persons: But in every nation he that feareth him, and worketh righteousness, is accepted with him.
Acts 10:34-35

While Peter yet spake these words, the Holy Ghost fell on all them which heard the word. And they of the circumcision which believed were astonished, as many as came with Peter, because that on the Gentiles also was poured out the gift of the Holy Ghost.
Acts 10:44-45

In fact, even after years of the new paradigm, Peter still struggled with his footing. Should he still stand on the old paradigm, or the new one? Should he put one foot on the old one and one on the new one? Peter's struggle was real, He didn't want to betray the brethren who still held to the old paradigm, a paradigm that had been in force for more than 2,000 years....by God's command!

But when Peter was come to Antioch, I withstood him to the face, because he was to be blamed. For before that certain came from James, he did eat with the Gentiles: but when they were come, he withdrew and separated himself, fearing them which were of the circumcision.· Galatians 2:11-12

This same issue is a struggle for the best of orthodox teachers today. When a person begins to study the book of Revelation, he must be prepared to get a glimpse of the new paradigm God has determined for this world. Good men like Brother Hank Hanegraaff are so focused on the orthodoxy of the old paradigm that they cannot handle the truths expressed in a book that points to a future paradigm. Inevitably, these orthodox ministers tend to make the book a metaphor of events and situations of the past. Although it's plain that the messages to the seven churches definitely refer to events of the early church period, it is equally plain that Revelation covers a timeframe throughout the church age, including future events involving Jerusalem, Babylon, and Rome. Therefore, many orthodox interpretations become vague and dissatisfying to the ardent student of Revelation. Plainly stated facts have to be relegated to Jewish idioms, and Jewish hyperbole. Much of the book has to simply be left to the ether of the past world in order to fit the old orthodoxy. In this chapter we intend to take a closer look at the "pricks" that goad us from the scriptures describing the new paradigm just ahead. I hope you're ready to leave the old paradigm behind, as we forge ahead into "what the Spirit saith unto the churches".

Perhaps the Book of Revelation repeats this admonition seven times in order to convince men that we must give heed to the Word He brings rather than cling to the ideas of the old paradigm. If you would like to take a clear, straight forward look at what the Spirit is saying in the book of Revelation, then fasten your seatbelts and hold on tight as we leave our comfortable paradigm for the one that is just ahead!

And no man putteth new wine into old bottles; else the new wine will burst the bottles, and be spilled, and the bottles shall perish. But new wine must be put into new bottles; and both are preserved. No man also having drunk old wine straightway desireth new: for he saith, The old is better. Luke 5:37-39

Preparing For Change

When Jesus and His disciples landed in the country of the Gadarenes, He was met by a couple of men whose lives were completely controlled by a host of demons. These men were possessed by demons of such strength and power that even bonds could not hold them, and no one could stop their attacks.

And when he was come to the other side into the country of the Gergesenes, there met him two possessed with devils, coming out of the tombs, exceeding fierce, so that no man might pass by that way. And, behold, they cried out, saying, What have we to do with thee, Jesus, thou Son of God? art thou come hither to torment us before the time? Matthew 8:28-29

When Jesus arrived on the other side of the lake in the land of the Gadarenes, men who were possessed by demons met him. They lived in a cemetery and were so dangerous that no one could go through that area. They began screaming at him, "Why are you bothering us, Son of God? You have no right to torture us before God's appointed time!" [NLT]

On this occasion, the tables were completely turned on these men. The men possessed of the demons came screaming and terrified to the feet of the master, crying out their recognition of His divinity. This was not an unusual response for demons in the presence of the Christ. And it was no different in this situation even though these men were possessed by a legion of the foul spirits. Perhaps the most notable thing about this encounter was the question cast at the savior's feet. One thing is abundantly clear from their exchange. These demons were aware of a divine timetable instituted by Almighty God; a timetable with set benchmarks already engraved by the creator of the universe. Perhaps equally intriguing is the fact that these demons, seemingly lowest in the rankings of the Kingdom of darkness, were yet fully aware of the "times" established by the self-existing one. It appears that information regarding God's timetable is common knowledge to the malevolent hosts aligned against His purposes, and those determined to overthrow His will.

Even the Prince of the Power of the air, is fully cognizant of the decrees of God.

Woe to the inhabiters of the earth and of the sea! for the devil is come down unto you, having great wrath, because he knoweth that he hath but a short time. Revelation 12:12

In light of our investigation into the coming paradigm shift described in the book of Revelation, this comes as a most enlightening piece of information. Not only is the Kingdom of Darkness aware of the coming paradigm shifts, but they are violently opposed to the prophesied outcomes! Nevertheless, we have it from God's own Word that a huge change is coming to the cosmos! Satan, who has ruled as the Prince of the Power of the air, is facing a coming moment when his entire following will be cast from our atmosphere and plunged into the earth! For some, perhaps, this vital information given to us by the Apostle Paul is of little consequence. Who cares if Satan is the prince of the power of our atmosphere.

Wherein in time past ye walked according to the course of this world, according to the prince of the power of the air, the spirit that now worketh in the children of disobedience: Ephesians 2:2

This "power" is a word denoting- force, authority, or jurisdiction. Without debate, Satan is the ruler, the absolute potentate of the atmosphere of earth. Of course, we know that he remains the prince only by God's permissive will, design and wisdom. Revelation is the unfolding of the story that details his ultimate dethronement and banishment to the lake of fire. The truth we have to take hold of here, is that the jurisdiction of our atmosphere is Satan's.

For we wrestle not against flesh and blood, but against principalities, against powers, against the rulers of the darkness of this world, against spiritual wickedness in high places. Ephesians 6:12

Do you recall how holy angels even met resistance from these satanic spirits ruling in earth's atmosphere?

Then said he unto me, Fear not, Daniel: for from the first day that thou didst set thine heart to understand, and to chasten thyself before thy God, thy words were heard, and I am come for thy words. But the prince of the kingdom of Persia withstood me one and twenty days: but, lo, Michael, one of the chief princes, came to help me; and I remained there with the kings of Persia.
Daniel 10:12-13

It's not hard to grasp the tremendous power and influence this spiritual kingdom of darkness holds over the lives and governments of men. Revelation pictures the intimate relationship between the kingdoms of man and Satan's kingdom with remarkable clarity.

And there appeared another wonder in heaven; and behold a great red dragon, having seven heads and ten horns, and seven crowns upon his heads. And his tail drew the third part of the stars of heaven, and did cast them to the earth: Revelation 12:3-4

Here we see Satan's kingdom symbolized as a great red dragon with 7 heads and 10 horns, and 7 crowns upon his head. This is also the symbol used of seven world empires of man on earth.

And I stood upon the sand of the sea, and saw a beast rise up out of the sea, having seven heads and ten horns, and upon his horns ten crowns, and upon his heads the name of blasphemy. And the beast which I saw was like unto a leopard, and his feet were as the feet oof a bear, and his mouth as the mouth of a lion: and the dragon gave him his power, and his seat, and great authority. Revelation13:1-2

The Old Testament bears witness to which empires the various beastly parts represent. They are the Grecian [leopard], Persian [bear], and Lion [Babylonian]. Here the world's seven kingdoms are all viewed as one beast. But what stands out most impressively, is that the dragon gives his own power and throne and authority to this succession of empires. The spiritual kingdom of darkness is totally identified with the government of man on this earth. This should come as no surprise since the human race yielded up his rightful dominion in the Garden of Eden. Interestingly, the coming paradigm shift will see a change this world has never seen before. For roughly six thousand years, Satan's kingdom has worked discreetly behind the scenes of man's governments. It's as if he has ruled the kingdoms of this world by "proxy". This will all change with the coming paradigm shift! And so, I repeat the scripture we quoted above.

And the great dragon was cast out, that old serpent, called the Devil, and Satan, which deceiveth the whole world: he was cast out into the earth, and his angels were cast out with him... Therefore rejoice, ye heavens, and ye that dwell in them. Woe to the inhabiters of the earth and of the sea! for the devil is come down unto you, having great wrath, because he knoweth that he hath but a short time. Revelation 12:9 &12

This may be a most difficult paradigm shift to swallow. But, the Word of God plainly states that a time is approaching when the very powers of heaven will be shaken and Satan and his fellow spirits will be cast out of the atmosphere and into the earth; at which time he has three and one half years to work his malice, before Christ returns to the earth. This "time" is clearly announced throughout the Old and New Testament. Even our Lord mentioned the events that would announce the moment of Satan's casting out of the atmosphere into the earth!

Immediately after the tribulation of those days shall the sun be darkened, and the moon shall not give her light, and the stars shall fall from heaven, and the powers of the heavens shall be shaken: Matthew 24:29

The careful reader of Revelation will see immediately that Christ is referring to the events taking place at the opening of the sixth seal. The description is identical. This is no metaphor, this is no hyperbole…this is reality! This great day of the Lord has been prophesied for ages. The powers of the heavens shall be shaken! Satan's kingdom will be thrust from the atmosphere into our earth!

And I beheld <u>when he had opened the sixth seal</u>, and, lo, there was a great earthquake; and the sun became black as sackcloth of hair, and the moon became as blood;   And the stars of heaven fell unto the earth, even as a fig tree casteth her untimely figs, when she is shaken of a mighty wind.   And the heaven departed as a scroll when it is rolled together; and every mountain and island were moved out of their places.*   <u>Revelation 6:12-14</u>

These events are unlike anything this world has ever seen or experienced. It is such a paradigm shift that the average man cannot readily assess the magnitude of this transformation of our world.   Satan will no longer rule this world through proxy governments.   The kingdoms of this world will come directly under his rule!   Entities that are alien to our own human race will seize control of the one world government of this world with absolute authority and power.   Although men will still be in office and still hold authority; supernatural, alien beings who have always ruled from the atmosphere, will suddenly be forced from their "high places" and will mingle with the seed of men.   The angel explained to Daniel about the final kingdom on earth before Christ comes:

And as the toes of the feet were part of iron, and part of clay, so the kingdom shall be partly strong, and partly broken.   And whereas thou sawest iron mixed with miry clay, they shall <u>mingle themselves with the seed of men</u>: but they shall not cleave one to another, even as iron is not mixed with clay. <u>Daniel 2:42-43</u>

These rulers will usurp unchallenged authority, because any attempt to thwart them is totally useless.

And they worshipped the dragon which gave power unto the beast: and they worshipped the beast, saying, <u>Who is like unto the beast?</u> <u>who is able to make war</u> with him?   And there was given unto him a mouth speaking great things and blasphemies; and power was given

76

unto him to continue forty and two months. And he opened his mouth in blasphemy against God, to blaspheme his name, and his tabernacle, and them that dwell in heaven. Revelation 13:4-6

After this I saw in the night visions, and behold a fourth beast, dreadful and terrible, and strong exceedingly; and it had great iron teeth: it devoured and brake in pieces, and stamped the residue with the feet of it: and it was diverse [different] from all the beasts [leaders] that were before it; and it had ten horns. I considered the horns, and, behold, there came up among them another little horn, before whom there were three of the first horns plucked up by the roots: and, behold, in this horn were eyes like the eyes of man, and a mouth speaking great things. Daniel 7:7-8

These beings and their leader will approach our world as "savior", and "Christ". They will arrive at a time when the earth's population will have been decimated by war, famine, and disease. Fully one third of mankind will have been killed by these plagues; meaning more than two billion people on the earth will have died. These creatures will offer hope and comfort for the devastated remnants of mankind. However, their main agenda, as outlined in the book of Revelation will be to completely rid the earth of all religion; every religious holiday, every religious custom, every religious gathering except to worship Satan's alien ruler. Read carefully the passages below.

And the sixth angel sounded, and I heard a voice from the four horns of the golden altar which is before God, Saying to the sixth angel which had the trumpet, Loose the four angels which are bound in the great river Euphrates. And the four angels were loosed, which were prepared for an hour, and a day, and a month, and a year, for to slay the third part of men. Revelation 9:13-15

And the ten horns out of this kingdom are ten kings that shall arise: and another shall rise after them; and he shall be diverse from the first, and he shall subdue three kings. And he shall speak great words against the most High, and shall wear out the saints of the most High, and think to change times and laws: and they shall be

given into his hand until a time and times and the dividing of time.
Daniel 7:24-25

These, my friends, are a description from God's own Word about the paradigm shift about to transform our very lives and planet. This is the paradigm that many foolish, unprepared Christians will be thrust into, as God's wrath begins to be poured out upon a world that has rebelled continuously against His will, and despised the only mediator given to secure their pardon. This paradigm is not only foretold over and over in the book of Daniel and in the book of Revelation, but it is seemingly even forecast by Satan's minions themselves. Men of science who have studied the ancient calendars of other civilizations have found a common theme advocated in one of the calendars from the Mayan Indians.

The Mayan's were totally consumed by occult, satanic worship. Their horrible rites of worship and government are well documented for all to see. Yet this diabolical society had satanically inspired calendars that ended with December in the year 2012. Although no Christian is going to put their confidence in a calendar originating from the dragon's very throne, we still get a glimpse of the demonic view of the times. One secular scholar commenting on the supposed purpose of the calendar's peculiar ending, could only surmise that it was purposeful, and that the Mayan's must have believed that the calendar portended some kind of colossal "paradigm shift" at that particular date in the future. One can only assume that at least in the halls of the kingdom of darkness, someone is looking forward to a moment in time when the kingdoms of this earth will become Satan's, as he attempts to work his own paradigm shift in the earth. Don't be fooled by old paradigms and think that these things cannot be. God's own word tells us:

And he shall speak great words against the most High, and shall wear out the saints of the most High, and think to change times and laws: and they shall be given into his hand until a time and times and the dividing of time. Daniel 7:25

For the mystery [secret plan] of iniquity doth already work: only he who now letteth [obstructs] *will let* [obstruct], *until he be taken out of the way. And then shall that Wicked be revealed, whom the Lord shall consume with the spirit of his mouth, and shall destroy with the brightness of his coming: Even him, whose coming is after the working of Satan with all power and signs and lying wonders, And with all deceivableness of unrighteousness in them that perish; because they received not the love of the truth, that they might be saved. And for this cause God shall send them strong delusion, that they should believe a lie: That they all might be damned who believed not the truth, but had pleasure in unrighteousness.*
II Thessalonians 2:7-12

For there shall arise false Christs, and false prophets, and shall shew great signs and wonders; insomuch that, if it were possible, they shall deceive the very elect. Matthew 24:24

Revelation gives us further insight into who these world rulers will be. These beings that are not "human beings".

And the fifth angel sounded, and I saw a star fall from heaven unto the earth: and to him was given the key of the bottomless pit. And he opened the bottomless pit; Revelation 9:1-2

And they had a king over them, which is the angel of the bottomless pit, whose name in the Hebrew tongue is Abaddon, but in the Greek tongue hath his name Apollyon Revelation 9:11

This creature is let loose from the bottomless pit in the earth, by Satan and becomes Satan's ruler on this earth. In fact, this creature is the only one capable, and permitted to kill the two witnesses that witness supernaturally for Christ at the end of this age.
And when they shall have finished their testimony, the beast that ascendeth out of the bottomless pit shall make war against them, and shall overcome them, and kill them. And their dead bodies shall lie in the street of the great city, which spiritually is called Sodom and Egypt, where also our Lord was crucified.
Revelation 11:7-8

It is at this point that the whole world is fully convinced that the two beasts that are not human, are indeed the world's savior and God! Further proof that Revelation is telling us of a time when alien, satanic creatures will rule this planet is evidenced by the description of their demise:

And the beast was taken, and with him the false prophet that wrought miracles before him, with which he deceived them that had received the mark of the beast, and them that worshipped his image. These both <u>were cast alive into a lake of fire burning with brimstone. And the remnant were slain with the sword</u> of him that sat upon the horse <u>Revelation 19:20-21</u>

Why do you suppose these two creatures are cast alive into the lake of fire, when it is appointed unto man, once to die and then the judgment [courtroom appearance]? These are not men! These are angelic creatures already judged by God in eons past! They are cast alive into the lake of fire for they cannot die, they are spirit beings. The rest of them are killed, as any ordinary human would be. Even Isaiah speaks of these spirit beings and the human kings of the earth dealt with at His coming:

The earth shall reel to and fro like a drunkard, and shall be removed like a cottage; and the transgression thereof shall be heavy upon it; and it shall fall, and not rise again. And it shall come to pass in that day, that <u>the LORD shall punish the host of the high ones that are on high, and the kings of the earth upon the earth.</u> And they shall be gathered together, as prisoners are gathered in the pit, and shall be shut up in the prison, and after many days shall they be visited. Then the moon shall be confounded, and the sun ashamed, when the LORD of hosts shall reign in mount Zion, and in Jerusalem, and before his ancients gloriously. <u>Isaiah 24:20-23</u>

Please do not dismiss these things as mere myth and fairytale. Although we have never experienced these kinds of things, they will happen. Scripture clearly shows that they have been kept back until the right moment when God will allow them to appear on our earth.

And the sixth angel sounded, and I heard a voice from the four horns of the golden altar which is before God, Saying to the sixth angel which had the trumpet, Loose the four angels which are bound in the great river Euphrates. And the four angels were loosed, <u>which were prepared for an hour, and a day, and a month, and a year,</u> for to slay the third part of men. <u>Revelation 9:13-15</u>

Allow Christ's warning to touch your heart with its full impact today!

And take heed to yourselves, lest at any time your hearts be overcharged with surfeiting, and drunkenness, and cares of this life, and so that day come upon you unawares. For as a snare shall it come on all them that dwell on the face of the whole earth. Watch ye therefore, and pray always, that ye may be accounted worthy to escape all these things that shall come to pass, and to stand before the Son of man. <u>Luke 21:34-36</u>

Prepare yourself to be a part of that triumphant company who will be redeemed from the earth at the time of the coming paradigm shift.

And there shall be signs in the sun, and in the moon, and in the stars; and upon the earth distress of nations, with perplexity; the sea and the waves roaring; Men's hearts failing them for fear, and for looking after those things which are coming on the earth: for the powers of heaven shall be shaken. And then shall they see the Son of man coming in a cloud with power and great glory. And when these things begin to come to pass, then look up, and lift up your heads; for <u>your redemption draweth nigh</u>. <u>Luke 21:25-28</u>

America

I think I can say, without debate, that the book of Revelation is one of the most challenging portions of the entire Bible. I think I can also say, that everything else about the book is entirely up for debate. Dr. Seiss, who wrote perhaps the quintessential exposition of the traditionally held futuristic interpretation of Revelation, passes on a tool that I find to be one of the most valuable tools available for the student of prophecy. Simply put, Dr. Seiss, firmly believed that a person should always look to scripture to interpret scripture. It's especially tempting to look outside of scripture for the meaning of things written in the book of Revelation. It seems like each generation can find things happening in current events that can be ascribed to various statements in the book. For example, someone may run across a reference to a dragon in the book of Revelation, and immediately suspect "China" to be an excellent choice for its proper interpretation, when indeed China has nothing to do with the matter discussed in the book. The same could be said about noticing a bear being mentioned in the book and ascribing it's meaning to be the Country of Russia since Russia is sometimes referred to as a bear. Using current events to interpret scripture is a sure way to get entangled in a boondoggle of misunderstanding. And so, I take you now to some Old Testament scriptures in order to interpret New Testament scripture recorded in the book of Revelation concerning a beast with 10 horns.

And I stood upon the sand of the sea, and saw a beast rise up out of the sea, having seven heads and ten horns, and upon his horns ten crowns, and upon his heads the name of blasphemy.
Revelation 13:1

In this chapter, I intend to delve into subject matter that may seem particularly relevant to current events, today. Be that as it may, let me say at the outset, that the things we will look at in this chapter were not put together for the purpose of making an application to current events. The material discovered in these verses merely surfaced as we used scripture to interpret scripture. What we discovered was as much a surprise to me as it may be to you. If so, be assured that the disciple of Christ can confidently stand, without fear, upon, "it is written". With this in mind, let's press on into an Old Testament book, the book of Daniel; a book given by God to show, not only Daniel, but all of His elect, the determinate counsel of God for the ages.

As you may know, God gave Daniel several visions concerning things that would happen after Daniel was deceased. More than one of these visions revealed to Daniel the various empires that would rise and fall before the last, and mightiest one would be crushed by God's anointed one, Jesus Christ. Daniel was faithful to disclose the things God revealed, even though at times he was totally confounded by the things he saw.

As for me Daniel, my cogitations much troubled me, and my countenance changed in me: but I kept the matter in my heart. Daniel 7:28

And I heard, but I understood not: then said I, O my Lord, what shall be the end of these things? And he said, Go thy way, Daniel: for the words are closed up and sealed till the time of the end. Daniel 12:8-9

This last injunction to Daniel was followed up by these words:

Many shall be purified, and made white, and tried; but the wicked shall do wickedly: and none of the wicked shall understand; but the wise shall understand. Daniel 12:10

This is a very insightful and hopeful message to those who are alive at "the end of these things". Evidently, God has every intention of revealing His will to those who are wise. Interestingly enough, Jesus divides the church into two groups at the end of the age in the parable of the wise and foolish virgins [Matthew 25]. Let us give every effort, and unrestrained energy to become those who worship Him in Spirit and truth, that we might be among the wise as we see the day approaching. For now, let's peer into one of those visions God gave to Daniel.

In the first year of Belshazzar king of Babylon Daniel had a dream and visions of his head upon his bed: then he wrote the dream, and told the sum of the matters. Daniel 7:1

As you read the account, you are swept up in the unfolding drama of four huge empires that would emerge on the world scene beginning with the empire that Daniel served under, the Babylonians.

And four great beasts came up from the sea, diverse one from another. Daniel 7:3

History reveals who those four empires were. We call them the Babylonian, the Persian, the Grecian, and the Roman Empires. Notably, the last empire, the Roman one, is revealed to succumb to a mortal wound, but then be revived later [Rev. 13] In fact, when it is revived, it comes forth as an empire ruled by a confederacy of 10 kings. It is this 10 king confederacy that opposes Christ at His second coming, and then is entirely demolished. Do you remember King Nebuchadnezzar's dream?

And in the second year of the reign of Nebuchadnezzar Nebuchadnezzar dreamed dreams, wherewith his spirit was troubled, and his sleep brake from him. Daniel 2:1

The king answered and said to Daniel, whose name was Belteshazzar, Art thou able to make known unto me the dream which I have seen, and the interpretation thereof? Daniel 2:26

Thou, O king, sawest, and behold a great image. This great image, whose brightness was excellent, stood before thee; and the form thereof was terrible. This image's head was of fine gold, his breast and his arms of silver, his belly and his thighs of brass, His legs of iron, his feet part of iron and part of clay. Thou sawest till that a stone was cut out without hands, which smote the image upon his feet that were of iron and clay, and brake them to pieces. Daniel 2:31-34

Each part of this great image represented a separate empire. Daniel recorded such fascinating, precise details about these empires, that many secular scholars believe the book of Daniel must have been written about the time of Jesus instead of five hundred years earlier. These unbelieving, secular writers fail to recognize that the fourth empire is the final revived Roman empire of this world which will be destroyed by Christ at his "future" second coming. When we take a close look at what the angel revealed to Daniel, a most amazing piece of evidence emerges to help us comprehend the things recorded by John in the book of Revelation. Let's look!

After this I saw in the night visions, and behold a fourth beast, dreadful and terrible, and strong exceedingly; and it had great iron teeth: it devoured and brake in pieces, and stamped the residue with the feet of it: and it was diverse from all the beasts that were before it; and it had ten horns. Daniel 7:7

Two things you will want to keep in mind as you compare this statement with statements made in the book of Revelation: First, it had ten horns. Secondly, it was different from all the beasts or kingdoms that came before it. If you recall, spiritual aliens are described in Revelation ruling on the earth at the time of the end. This is no doubt why we read it was "diverse from all the beasts that were before it". The world-wide government at the end of the age is led by beings from our atmosphere and the bottomless pit. They are "spiritual" entities that will be cast into the earth according to Revelation 12, and, they will also ascend from the bottomless pit!

Just as it will be a time for God to glorify the first fruits that are his, giving them a physical body, merged with a spiritual one; so will it be with the counterfeit kingdom of the Dragon, that old serpent the Devil. Of course, everything Satan attempts is a lie and a fraud, and this will be no different. The merged spirit entities in flesh will not spring from truth, but they will greatly impact the beliefs of most people.

For the mystery of iniquity doth already work: only he who now letteth [obstructs] will let [obstruct], until he be taken out of the way. And then shall that Wicked be revealed, whom the Lord shall

consume with the spirit of his mouth, and shall destroy with the brightness of his coming: Even him, whose coming is after the working of Satan with all power and signs and lying wonders, And with all deceivableness of unrighteousness in them that perish; because they received not the love of the truth, that they might be saved. And for this cause God shall send them strong delusion, that they should believe a lie: That they all might be damned who believed not the truth, but had pleasure in unrighteousness.
II Thessalonians 2:11-12

Daniel was mesmerized by the vision of the final beast. It was unlike any other beast that was shown to him. He was so amazed by the final beast that he asked one of the angels to help him understand more about that final beast rising up on the earth.

I Daniel was grieved in my spirit in the midst of my body, and the visions of my head troubled me. I came near unto one of them that stood by, and asked him the truth of all this. So he told me, and made me know the interpretation of the things. These great beasts, which are four, are four kings, which shall arise out of the earth. But the saints of the most High shall take the kingdom, and possess the kingdom for ever, even for ever and ever.
Daniel 7:15-18

Now this is great news! Although the strongest and most evil of all empires will rule during the last 3 ½ years before Christ returns, we are assured by God's Word that we will possess the Kingdom eternally! Yes, the meek do inherit the earth! But, Daniel wanted to know more about this final beast.

Then I would know the truth of the fourth beast, which was diverse from all the others, exceeding dreadful, whose teeth were of iron, and his nails of brass; which devoured, brake in pieces, and stamped the residue with his feet; And of the ten horns that were in his head, and of the other which came up, and before whom three fell; even of that horn that had eyes, and a mouth that spake very great things, whose look was more stout than his fellows.
Daniel 7:19-20

Daniel was taken aback by the invincible strength and power of this final beast. It must have been a relief to see that God would deal with the creature himself, since no man seemed able to withstand his will.

I beheld, and the same horn made war with the saints, and prevailed against them; Until the Ancient of days came, and judgment was given to the saints of the most High; and the time came that the saints possessed the kingdom. Daniel 7:21-22

Then the Angel continued:

Thus he said, The fourth beast shall be the fourth kingdom upon earth, which shall be diverse from all kingdoms, and shall devour the whole earth, and shall tread it down, and break it in pieces. And the ten horns out of this kingdom are ten kings that shall arise: and another shall rise after them; and he shall be diverse from the first, and he shall subdue three kings. Daniel 7:23-24

Once again emphasizing the extreme difference between this kingdom and former ones on the earth; and the extreme difference between this ruler and all former ones on the earth, the angel makes it clear to Daniel that the final empire was not of this world. Instead, this alien will go about to change the earthly paradigm completely.

And he shall speak great words against the most High, and shall wear out the saints of the most High, and think to change times and laws: and they shall be given into his hand until a time and times and the dividing of time. But the judgment shall sit, and they shall take away his dominion, to consume and to destroy it unto the end. Daniel 7:25-26

As always, God has the final word about all matters big and small, and the dominion of the beast is taken away while its rulers are destroyed! Hallelujah!

And the kingdom and dominion, and the greatness of the kingdom

87

under the whole heaven, shall be given to the people of the saints of the most High, whose kingdom is an everlasting kingdom, and all dominions shall serve and obey him. Daniel 7:27

At this point, I want to ask you to compare two separate statements spoken by the angel. The two statements are very similar, but the difference is of vast importance to our clear understanding of things recorded in the book of Revelation. Compare these two statements:

These great beasts, which are four, are four kings, which shall arise out of the earth. Daniel 7:17

Thus he said, The fourth beast shall be the fourth kingdom upon earth, which shall be diverse from all kingdoms, and shall devour the whole earth, Daniel 7:23

Do you see the difference between these two verses? It may be a subtle difference, but it makes a huge difference in our understanding of the book of Revelation. At first, the angel says the beasts are four KINGS, and then he says a beast is a KINGDOM. This is not a form of trickery, nor is it simply a man-made delineation. This is God's Word, and the interpretation given by the angel. From these statements, we can gather conclusively, that these beasts represent both the King and his Kingdom. In some instances, the author may be referring to the entire Kingdom. In some others, he may be referring specifically to the leader. In fact, it is feasible that at times the author means to identify both the Kingdom and it's King. But, the fact remains that a beast represents either a King or his Kingdom. Naturally, the history books have recorded these beasts as "empires" not "Kingdoms". Whereas, most nations have had "kings" in the past, now most nations have a president or prime minister or some other supreme ruler. Using a more contemporary usage to interpret these beasts, we would, no doubt, say something like: "they represent a country and its leader."

Having seen this interpretation given by the angel of God, let us move on to the book of Revelation where John also was given a glimpse of this final beast. God shared some more details with John about this very same beast with the ten horns. The biggest difference being that John saw a beast with seven heads instead of a single one like Daniel saw. The obvious reason as described in the context is that God is symbolizing to John, all seven of the various empires that have ruled over the known earth surrounding the Mediterranean Sea, whereas, Daniel was shown four of those empires separately and each was symbolized by a different beast. Interestingly, the first three beasts in Daniel were symbolized by a lion, bear, and a leopard; the exact same "makeup" of the beast shown to John.

And I stood upon the sand of the sea, and saw a beast rise up out of the sea, having seven heads and ten horns, and upon his horns ten crowns, and upon his heads the name of blasphemy. And the beast which I saw was like unto a leopard, and his feet were as the feet of a bear, and his mouth as the mouth of a lion: and the dragon gave him his power, and his seat, and great authority. Revelation 13:1-2

At this point in God's disclosure to us, we discover that the fourth beast will start off as the Roman Empire of old. However, it will be mortally wounded and yet miraculously recover at the end of the age under the direction of the 10 horns [kings]

And I saw one of his heads as it were wounded to death; and his deadly wound was healed: and all the world wondered after the beast. And they worshipped the dragon which gave power unto the beast: and they worshipped the beast, saying, Who is like unto the beast? who is able to make war with him? Revelation 13:3-4

Practically everywhere a reference is made to this fourth and final beast, it is only spoken of in the context of its final "revived" condition. For those who may not know, the European Union of today was initially begun by the Treaties of Rome in 1957. This great union of European nations has over 25 members, and yet only ten of the members are considered to have "full" membership. The other nations have only "associate" membership, according to "Contender Ministries" of England. These original ten members are considered to be the "10 Nation Military Wing of the Union". The formation of the union has been a slow process beginning with agreements made for commerce, then agriculture, and finally a political union. At the time of this writing, except for a couple of holdouts, all the members have ratified the establishment of a single, centralized government. One of their posters frequently used to promote the European Union is a picture of the ancient tower of Babel being reconstructed with cranes and these words written in big letters: "Europe, many tongues, one voice". [see the internet] In other writings we will discuss Revelation chapters 17 and 18 which discuss in detail the utter destruction of "Babylon".

To summarize the points we have discovered so far in the scriptures, we see that the end of the age will result in an empire that is a combination of ten leaders and their nations joining together. We realize that a beast is a symbol of an empire and its leader. We see that the prophesied antichrist will arise as the super leader of this entity and oppose Christ, himself!

After this I saw in the night visions, and behold a fourth beast, dreadful and terrible, and strong exceedingly; and it had great iron teeth: it devoured and brake in pieces, and stamped the residue with the feet of it: and it was diverse from all the beasts that were before it; and it had ten horns. I considered the horns, and, behold, there came up among them another little horn, before whom there were three of the first horns plucked up by the roots: and, behold, in this horn were eyes like the eyes of man, and a mouth speaking great things. Daniel 7:7-8

We are definitely not alone in viewing the EU as the very formation of this fourth and final beast. At times, the scriptures make reference to the empire as "the beast", and at times scriptures make reference to the leader himself as "the beast". Although a host of authors and theologians might agree that the EU is indeed this very beast revealed in Daniel 7 and in Revelation 13, not a single writer I know, carries this same interpretation of a beast down to verse 11 in chapter 13.

And I beheld another beast coming up out of the earth; and he had two horns like a lamb, and he spake as a dragon. And he exerciseth all the power of the first beast before him, and causeth the earth and them which dwell therein to worship the first beast, whose deadly wound was healed. Revelation 13:11-12

Here, in no uncertain terms, we find a second beast upon the scene of the final 3 ½ years of the age. The students who would stay true to scripture; allowing scripture to interpret scripture, would find themselves contemplating a second country with its leader at the end of this age, or "generation" as Jesus once put it.

Verily I say unto you, This generation [age] shall not pass, till all these things be fulfilled. Matthew 24:34

For the most part, theologians, eschatologists, and authors have preferred to view this second beast as a mere man; a man who is above all else, a false prophet. The common consensus being that he represents some religious leader at the end of the age who will work in conjunction with the antichrist to deceive the nations.

And the beast was taken, and with him the false prophet that wrought miracles before him, with which he deceived them that had received the mark of the beast, and them that worshipped his image. These both were cast alive into a lake of fire burning with brimstone. Revelation 19:20

Although, it is apparent that some of these conclusions may bear the weight of scripture, I for one am not ready to throw out the interpretation given by the angel when he interpreted the meaning of a beast. Without objection, we should be free to interpret this second beast of Revelation to be a country and its leader. This becomes even more profound as we begin to read what this beast is like and his role at the end of the age.

And I beheld another beast coming up out of the earth; and he had two horns like a lamb, and he spake as a dragon. Revelation 13:1

Breaking this down, we notice first of all that this beast comes up out of the earth. This is significantly different than the first beast whose origination came from the existing nations of the old world… or "the sea". By contrast, this country comes up from somewhere other than those nations. It appears to just appear out of nowhere. This may be a description of our own beloved United States of America. Early colonists arrived from the old world and eventually just set up a nation over here.

Secondly, the country we are contemplating had two horns like a lamb. There could be a couple of reasons for this symbolism. But, before we rush to judgment on its meaning, let's look at the Old Testament for an understanding of what horns represented upon the beasts that Daniel saw.

Then I lifted up mine eyes, and saw, and, behold, there stood before the river a ram which had two horns: and the two horns were high; but one was higher than the other: and the higher came up last. Daniel 8:3

Practically every commentator agrees that this is a picture of the Medo-Persian empire that swept away the Babylonian empire in a single night. The accuracy of their description is precise. The kingdom was ruled by the Medes at the beginning, but the Persians, who became a much greater dynasty, began to rule secondly. A verse or two later depicts the advancing Grecian empire rising up under their leader, Alexander the Great, as he come to overthrow the Persian Empire.

And as I was considering, behold, an he goat came from the west on the face of the whole earth, and touched not the ground: and the goat had a notable horn between his eyes. And he came to the ram that had two horns, which I had seen standing before the river, and ran unto him in the fury of his power. Daniel 8:5-6

Even a novice can see that the use of these horns is very precise in description in order to give an accurate symbol of the Rule, Authority, and Dominion of these various empires. Later, even the horn of Alexander the Great was broken and replaced by four notable horns. History tells us that his four generals split up his kingdom into four separate kingdoms.

Therefore the he goat waxed very great: and when he was strong, the great horn was broken; and for it came up four notable ones toward the four winds of heaven. Daniel 8:8

With this in mind, let us return to the book of Revelation to see what might be understood about this final beast at the end of the age who has two horns like a lamb. If you've ever studied a chart of the end times, you no doubt have seen a picture portraying this "beast with two horns like a lamb". I certainly have seen some pictures. Much to my surprise, the drawings of the lamb looked much more like a goat standing on its hind feet and sporting two giant horns like a Billy goat. Curiosity getting the best of me, I looked up the Greek word for "lamb", and discovered it meant simply a very young, tender lamb. I'm not sure lambs even have horns. But, if they do, I'm certain they are very insignificant and not designed to tear down and destroy others; unlike the beasts we saw from the Old Testament. One could say that, symbolically, the character of this "lamb" nation might be very gentle and benign as it relates to the countries around it. America has always been a very benevolent country, giving billions of dollars to restore and re-establish it's defeated foes i.e. Germany, Japan, and more recently Iraq. Add to this idea the fact that Revelation portrays Jesus as a lamb in Revelation chapter 5.

And I beheld, and, lo, in the midst of the throne and of the four beasts, and in the midst of the elders, stood a Lamb as it had been slain, Revelation 5:6

One may be inclined to think that the country laid out before us in Chapter 13 is being presented as a Christian nation. If so, keep in mind that America is the only nation in the world that was actually established as a Christian Nation.   In spite of the Christian symbolism for this final country mentioned in Revelation, we can't help but take note of the symbolism for its mouthpiece, or leader, if you will.

...and he spake as a dragon.   Revelation 13:11

We're all probably familiar with the "dragon" of Revelation, who is identified as none other than Satan himself!

And the great dragon was cast out, that old serpent, called the Devil, and Satan, which deceiveth the whole world: he was cast out into the earth, and his angels were cast out with him. Revelation 12:9

Obviously, there is something sinister about the leader of this final country before Christ returns.   We discovered earlier that he is not a human being, but rather an angelic ruler from the kingdom of Darkness.   Not only does the symbolism speak of one empowered by Satan, but also as one who is invincible.   The mythical dragons were always held as unconcerned about, and above the attacks of men since they were covered in a layer of thick scales.   Here too, we are, no doubt, envisioning one who has no weakness when confronting the powers of earthly men.

As a further point about this symbolic beast, it had two horns; not one, not four, not three, but two.   Relying on the preciseness of God's picture to us, let me remind you that America has always had a two party ruling government.   We have had more than two parties, but two have always held the power, rule, and dominion.

Next we find that this final nation works in conjunction with the first beast, and has the very same power as the first one as well.   Just a little research shows us that the two beasts are getting their power supernaturally, for the Dragon [Satan] gives them their power.
And he exerciseth all the power of the first beast before him, and causeth the earth and them which dwell therein to worship the first beast, whose deadly wound was healed. Revelation 13:12

94

Sadly, if this final nation turns out to be America, we find it being run by a being that is not human. Instead, he is a foul agent of the Kingdom of Darkness just as the leader of the ten nation empire is. The two work hand-in-hand to bring the entire world to serve and follow the dictates of the antichrist who will then rule over the revived Roman empire which we call, the European Union! As Christ warned the disciples, he will make every effort to deceive the human race into thinking antichrist is indeed the savior of the world through the implementation of fraudulent use of superior power.

And he doeth great wonders, so that he maketh fire come down from heaven on the earth in the sight of men, And deceiveth them that dwell on the earth by the means of those miracles which he had power to do in the sight of the beast; Revelation 13:13-14

Although America already possesses the ability to call fire down from heaven in the sight of men via the missiles delivered through the air, it seems that this malignant leader will do far more electrifying performances with his advanced, superior technology; which he delivers in conjunction with the antichrist of the European Union. In fact, he will go so far as to compel the entire world to line up with some form of representative body under the antichrist's thumb. This could very well be the body we now know as the United Nations.

...saying to them that dwell on the earth, that they should make an image [representative body] to the beast, which had the wound by a sword, and did live. And he had power to give life unto the image of the beast, that the image of the beast should both speak, and cause that as many as would not worship the image of the beast should be killed. Revelation 13:14-15

Without appearing boastful, America has already proven to be the main "mover and shaker" behind the will of the U.N. Under the future leader of America, it appears that the whole world will have to serve the beast via the U.N. or face the consequences. This is not hard to fathom when you take under consideration the state of the world at the time of these two final beasts. The world will have just experienced another global war which will have caused the death of 1/3 of the earth's population.

And the sixth angel sounded, and I heard a voice from the four horns of the golden altar which is before God, Saying to the sixth angel which had the trumpet, Loose the four angels which are bound in the great river Euphrates. And the four angels were loosed, which were prepared for an hour, and a day, and a month, and a year, for to slay the third part of men.   Revelation 9:13-15

No doubt, the majority of the earth's population will find great comfort in these outsiders who come to save us from ourselves. They might even find the capstone of their plan to be quite ingenious!

And he causeth all, both small and great, rich and poor, free and bond, to receive a mark in their right hand, or in their foreheads: And that no man might buy or sell, save he that had the mark, or the name of the beast, or the number of his name. Here is wisdom. Let him that hath understanding count the number of the beast: for it is the number of a man; and his number is Six hundred threescore and six.   Revelation 13:16-18

Again, although America already possesses technology to either insert micro-chips, or an invisible tattoo capable of transmitting a radio signal into the skin of man, it appears that the coming leaders will use some form of technology to absolutely create a brand new financial system totally under the control of the leadership of the one world government!   It's interesting, that as I write this in February 2009, our world is facing the imminent, total dismantling of the world's financial systems.   Could it be, that the next financial system prepared for this world will be the one we've all heard so much about through the centuries; the one enumerated by the numbers 666.

Hopefully, the second beast of Revelation is not a reference to our beloved United States of America.   But, if it is referring to some other nation at the end of the age, what nation in this world fits the description given to us by Revelation 13 nearly as close as the United States of America? Indeed, what other country even comes close? As appealing as the solutions offered by these aliens may seem, after experiencing such devastation, death and disease; the admonition of our Lord is stated quite plainly.

And the third angel followed them, saying with a loud voice, <u>If any</u> <u>*man worship the beast and his image, and receive his mark in his*</u> <u>*forehead, or in his hand, The same shall drink of the wine of the*</u> <u>*wrath of God,*</u> *which is poured out without mixture into the cup of his indignation; and he shall be tormented with fire and brimstone in the presence of the holy angels, and in the presence of the Lamb: And the smoke of their torment ascendeth up for ever and ever: and they have no rest day nor night, who worship the beast and his image, and whosoever receiveth the mark of his name.* Revelation 14:9-11

God leaves us no doubt about His opinion of the beast that blasphemes Him for three and one half years. It will be a time where no one will continue in a lukewarm condition. Everyone will either choose God and redemption through His only begotten Son, or they will choose the ultimate imposter who will come to deceive all that he can.

For there shall arise false Christs, and false prophets, and shall shew great signs and wonders; insomuch that, if it were possible, they shall deceive the very elect. Behold, I have told you before. Matthew 24:24-25·

It should stir our souls, even to the point that we give diligent heed to the master's warning:

For as a snare shall it come on all them that dwell on the face of the whole earth. Watch ye therefore, and pray always, that ye may be accounted worthy to escape all these things that shall come to pass, and to stand before the Son of man. Luke 21:35-36 AMEN!

At the time of this writing, the events of the seven seals have not yet been unleashed. However, the signs of our time point increasingly to a literal and sudden fulfillment of these things. Once they are set in motion, once the first seal is unsealed, there will be no turning back until Christ reigns in the earth! And what is that first seal that indicates to one and all that God is moving to answer the prayers of the saints? It will be the moment radical Islamic leaders initiate their world-wide attempt to bring down the governments of this world through "Holy Jihad". Pure hell will ensue for the next several years as nations rise against nation. The earth will be filled with wars and rumors of wars. Inflation and starvation will grip whole continents. Martial law will be established in virtually every country as multitudes of people burst into anarchy and hatred. Death and disease will stalk the nations unabated. And then, in God's perfect time, the 6th seal will be loosed. The heavens will depart like a scroll rolling together. The entire earth will quake. Meteorites will cascade down upon men, as volcanoes erupt sporadically about the globe. Tsunamis will crash against many great port cities. Men's hearts will fail them for fear as they see all this coming upon the earth. The great day of God's wrath will have begun.

And there shall be signs in the sun, and in the moon, and in the stars; and upon the earth distress of nations, with perplexity; the sea and the waves roaring; Men's hearts failing them for fear, and for looking after those things which are coming on the earth: for the powers of heaven shall be shaken. Luke 21:25-26

Supernatural changes will go into effect immediately. The first fruits unto God and the Lamb will suddenly become "glorified" saints in their new bodies. Jesus' two witnesses will appear in the earth with supernatural ability to wreak havoc upon the earth, and begin a special witness for Christ to the unbelieving nation of Israel, with the goal of converting them or completely destroying the land of Israel again.

And his disciples asked him, saying, Why then say the scribes that Elias must first come? And Jesus answered and said unto them, Elias truly shall first come, and restore all things. Matthew 17:10

Behold, I will send you Elijah the prophet before the great and awesome day of the LORD comes. And he will turn the hearts of fathers to their children and the hearts of children to their fathers, lest I come and strike the land with a decree of utter destruction. Malachi 4:5-6

Satan and his angels will be cast from the atmosphere, where they currently reside, into the earth, with the ability to take some type of physical form. He too will harbor great wrath, as he knows his time is short. The foolish saints will have to flee into the wilderness or face imprisonment or death at the hands of the New Diabolical World Government. Three and a half years of extreme difficulty will "try" the inhabitants of the world, until finally the harvest will come at the sound of the last trumpet. The dead in Christ shall rise first, and then we which are alive and remain will be caught up together to meet the Lord in the air. The beast, that is "proven" to be mightier than Christ's two witnesses, will convince the world that he alone is almighty. The advancing armies of the world, under the persuasive supernatural strength of the antichrist, will turn their fire power upon the descending hosts of heaven, convinced that they are aliens coming to destroy the earth. Christ and his saints will surge down riding on some kind of craft [white horses] in perfect unity destroying all that oppose the King of Kings, and Lord of Lords. Then Christ and his saints will begin a rule of a thousand years bringing peace and prosperity once again to a planet restored to the original bliss of the paradise that was lost. And what does Christ tell us?

And when these things begin to come to pass, then look up, and lift up your heads; for your redemption draweth nigh. Luke 21:28

For as a snare shall it come on all them that dwell on the face of the whole earth. Watch ye therefore, and pray always, that ye may be accounted worthy to escape all these things that shall come to pass, and to stand before the Son of man. Luke 21:35-36

And what is the response of the wise and waiting child of God?

And the Spirit and the bride say, Come. And let him that heareth say, Come. And let him that is athirst come. And whosoever will, let him take the water of life freely. For I testify unto every man that heareth the words of the prophecy of this book, If any man shall add unto these things, God shall add unto him the plagues that are written in this book: And if any man shall take away from the words of the book of this prophecy, God shall take away his part out of the book of life, and out of the holy city, and from the things which are written in this book. He which testifieth these things saith, Surely I come quickly. Amen. Even so, come, Lord Jesus. The grace of our Lord Jesus Christ be with you all. Amen.
Revelation 22:17-20

And so, dear child of God, as we move into the final coming years of this generation, be advised by our Lord:

And Jesus answered and said unto them, Take heed that no man deceive you. For many shall come in my name, saying, I am Christ; and shall deceive many. And ye shall hear of wars and rumours of wars: see that ye be not troubled: for all these things must come to pass, but the end is not yet.   Matthew 24:4-6

We must not ignore what the James told us even though we enter into this special time of travail:

My brethren, count it all joy when ye fall into divers temptations; Knowing this, that the trying of your faith worketh patience. But let patience have her perfect work, that ye may be perfect and entire, wanting nothing.   James 2 - 3

The time of "travail" is approaching. The church will begin to experience some very hard labor pains, and birth contractions. We are not to panic, for all these things must come to pass. We must see this for what it is; an opportunity for delayed "Joy", that is, our glorification. Therefore, we can count it "joy" even as the travail is upon us. In God's wisdom, the church is being given one last opportunity to cry out to God for deliverance. Out of this cry a "manchild" will be delivered and caught up to the throne of God to begin ruling and reigning in a way only Christ has experienced. From this painful time ahead will emerge the glorious and triumphant "first fruits" unto God and the Lamb. Joy unspeakable [beyond description] and full(ness) of GLORY is just ahead for the travailing, overcoming saint of God. So, do not despair at the coming days of hardship. Instead view every difficulty, every increasing pressure of life, every failing of the flesh to be one thing and one thing only.... Your REDEMPTION!!

And when these things begin to come to pass, then look up [in anticipation], and lift up your heads [in victory]; for your redemption draweth nigh. <u>Luke 21:28</u>

And, what should we do to prepare for these things? As always the instructions of our master are plain and simple. They are summed up in two words alone; watch and Pray! We must not become swallowed up with the normal affairs of life. We must remain vigilant. Our enemy wants to overwhelm us with the cares of life and the deceitfulness of riches. He wants every bit of our oil [communion with Christ] to be drained from our life. He wants to entice us with every possible pleasure, diversion, and lust, to veer away from holiness. Christ says, we must remain vigilant, and we must stay in communion with him. And above all, keep yourselves pure.

We know that, when he shall appear, we shall be like him; for we shall see him as he is. And every man that hath this hope in him purifieth himself, even as he is pure. <u>I John 3:2-3</u>

TRANSFORMED

As we hurtle towards the conclusion of the heart cries of the saints of all ages… "thy kingdom come, thy will be done on earth as it is in heaven", let us never forget for a moment the heart cry of God as well:

And the Spirit and the bride say, Come. And let him that heareth say, Come. And let him that is athirst come. And whosoever will, let him take the water of life freely.
Revelation 22:17

He which testifieth these things saith, Surely I come quickly. Amen. Even so, come, Lord Jesus. Revelation 22:20

The coming paradigm shift will strike this whole world as no other paradigm has ever done. This earth will witness things never before seen. Horrors unimagined will engulf the whole planet. Wars of unimaginable destruction will inundate the planet. Chaos, death and destruction will seem unstoppable. Hunger, disease and death will be the norm for billions of people. Beings from outside our normal perception will not only confront the world, but absolutely rule the world. The pundits of this world will unanimously agree that these agents are our salvation and recourse for obtaining long awaited "PEACE". Christians will be forced to take a stand for Christ or for this world, as all religion will be literally outlawed and devoured upon this earth.

And the angel said to me, "The waters where the prostitute is sitting represent masses of people of every nation and language. The scarlet beast and his ten horns—which represent ten kings who will reign with him—all hate the prostitute. They will strip her naked, eat her flesh, and burn her remains with fire. For God has put a plan into their minds; a plan that will carry out his purposes. They will mutually agree to give their authority to the scarlet beast, and so the words of God will be fulfilled.
Revelation 17:15-17

Future writings may disclose more on Chapter 17 and "Mystery Babylon". However, this rampage against God's people will lead many to death or to imprisonment. God encourages us not to despair.

If any man have an ear, let him hear. He that leadeth into captivity shall go into captivity: he that killeth with the sword must be killed with the sword. Here is the patience and the faith of the saints. Revelation 13:9-10

Others will flee into the wilderness to dwell apart from the nations of this world. But, Just as it seems that no other solution is possible upon this earth; just as the one world government defeats the final, standing opponents to this "new world order"; just as all seems lost and hopeless for those who have remained true to the living God of the Bible in the face of overwhelming "proof" that no such God exists; just as Jesus and his claims are made out to be a total buffoon…Suddenly.

And then shall appear the sign of the Son of man in heaven: and then shall all the tribes of the earth mourn, and they shall see the Son of man coming in the clouds of heaven with power and great glory. And he shall send his angels with a great sound of a trumpet, and they shall gather together his elect from the four winds, from one end of heaven to the other. Matthew 24:30-31

The two special witnesses for Christ will be lying dead in the streets of Jerusalem. The world will be rejoicing thinking, "finally, peace and safety" when without warning the unthinkable will happen before the very eyes of this rebellious world.

And when they [the two witnesses] *shall have finished their testimony, the beast that ascendeth out of the bottomless pit shall make war against them, and shall overcome them, and kill them. And their dead bodies shall lie in the street of the great city, which spiritually is called Sodom and Egypt, where also our Lord was crucified. And they of the people and kindreds and tongues and nations shall see their dead bodies three days and an half, and shall*

103

not suffer their dead bodies to be put in graves. And they that dwell upon the earth shall rejoice over them, and make merry, and shall send gifts one to another; because these two prophets tormented them that dwelt on the earth. And after three days and an half the Spirit of life from God entered into them, and they stood upon their feet; and great fear fell upon them which saw them. And they heard a great voice from heaven saying unto them, Come up hither. And they ascended up to heaven in a cloud; and their enemies beheld them. And the same hour was there a great earthquake, and the tenth part of the city fell, and in the earthquake were slain of men seven thousand: and the remnant were affrighted, and gave glory to the God of heaven. Revelation 11:7-13

In light of these testimonies given by God, where should your attention and interest be this hour?   With what should your life be consumed?   Making   a   living?   Preparing   for   retirement? Concerned primarily with a fluctuating stock market? Disputing with your neighbors and fellow workers?   Pursuing the pleasures of life and the entertainments that abound?   God the creator of heaven and earth has invited you to share in eternal glory with him.   He's inclined to come and indwell you now by His Holy Spirit; and He's inclined to transform you into an eternal being with a glorified body. All He asks for is your heart in exchange.

Jesus said unto him, Thou shalt love the Lord thy God with all thy heart, and with all thy soul, and with all thy mind.   This is the first and great commandment. And the second is like unto it, Thou shalt love thy neighbour as thyself.   Matthew 22:37-39

His posture toward you today is shown in Revelation 3:20-22

Behold, I stand at the door, and knock: if any man hear my voice, and open the door, I will come in to him, and will sup with him, and he with me. To him that overcometh will I grant to sit with me in my throne, even as I also overcame, and am set down with my Father in his throne.   He that hath an ear, let him hear what the Spirit saith unto the churches.

Unfortunately, we are being swamped by a flood of New Age ideas that include the idea that man is actually God within. More and more political, educational, and religious leaders are anticipating a great initiation of the residents of earth into a great awareness of our own godhood. Even Christianity is being influenced by ideas that would make it seem the Bible, itself, looks forward to the day that man will become "creator" himself. The truth remains however that although God intends to give us eternal life; and though he intends to give us a seat of authority with him; there still remains only one self-existing creator, and He is the God of the Bible.

Prepare yourself for counterfeits and frauds as we approach the time of the end. Every conceivable method will be utilized to rip the very idea of a sovereign God, the God of the Bible, from your heart and mind. Get to know Him personally, now! And make every effort to grow in that personal relationship with Him daily. Why… because the moment for gathering the first fruits appears to be drawing very close.

And take heed to yourselves, lest at any time your hearts be overcharged with surfeiting, and drunkenness, and cares of this life, and so that day come upon you unawares. For as a snare shall it come on all them that dwell on the face of the whole earth. Watch ye therefore, and pray always, that ye may be accounted worthy to escape all these things that shall come to pass, and to stand before the Son of man. Luke 21:34-36

A certain "worthiness" is required for those who would be in the first fruits company of believers. Although, a holy, sanctified life is one of those pre-requisites, and a supreme love for God as well, perhaps a real-life example would help us understand why it is so vital to be counted worthy at the time of this transformation. Do you recall the time that Jesus himself was glorified while he was here on earth? His disciples remembered it well.

And after six days Jesus taketh Peter, James, and John his brother, and bringeth them up into an high mountain apart, And was transfigured before them: and his face did shine as the sun, and his raiment was white as the light. Matthew 17:1-2

And the Word was made flesh, and dwelt among us, (and we beheld his glory, the glory as of the only begotten of the Father,) full of grace and truth. John 1:14

Here we see our savior being transformed or "glorified". Everything about him glistened at this moment. What do you suppose was happening to his body at that moment. Although I am no scientist, and though we are not given an explanation of how this happened. Modern science has come far enough along to know a little bit about the atoms that make up our physical world. They also understand more and more about light waves, sound waves, and electro-magnetic waves in general. The vibrations of these waves can vary enormously, determining what we can see and not see; what we can hear and not hear. We know that light is also made of vibrations as well. Somehow it seems that the Spirit of God, which was totally engaged with Christ, suddenly began to vibrate the very atoms of Christ's body. I believe that this same type of vibration coming from the Spirit of God will one day transform [glorify] the very bodies of God's people. The saints who are "engaged" with the Spirit of God at that moment can then be glorified. Those who, for various reasons, are not engaged [out of oil] will not be able to be glorified at that time.

Another appropriate illustration might be a set of gears. We've all seen gears that mesh together as they rotate. One gear has power behind it and drives the gears that come into contact with the notches on its perimeter. Likewise, the saints that are in spiritual contact with the Holy Spirit at the time He intends to "vibrate" them, will experience the power of the Holy Spirit to be transformed. It behooves us that are waiting for his appearing to be sure that our lives are full of the oil [the Holy Spirit]. We must be sure that our spirit is engaged with his Spirit in order for the transformation to "take". Perhaps this is why our Lord tells some in the church…*Afterward came also the other virgins, saying, Lord, Lord, open to us. But he answered and said, Verily I say unto you, I know you not.* Matthew 25:11

We've got to be personally connected to him!

And so we repeat:

Watch ye therefore, and pray always, that ye may be accounted worthy to escape all these things that shall come to pass, and to stand before the Son of man. [GLORIFIED, REDEEMED]
Luke 21:34-36

May God speed the day of this tremendous, long-awaited, paradigm shift!   May he grant each of us the singleness of heart to prepare for its long-awaited inauguration, and may we greet him with pure hearts, and wearing a white robe of righteousness. Amen!

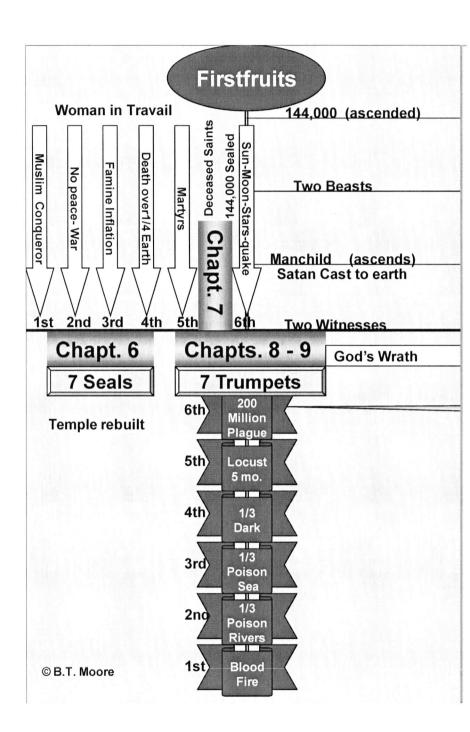

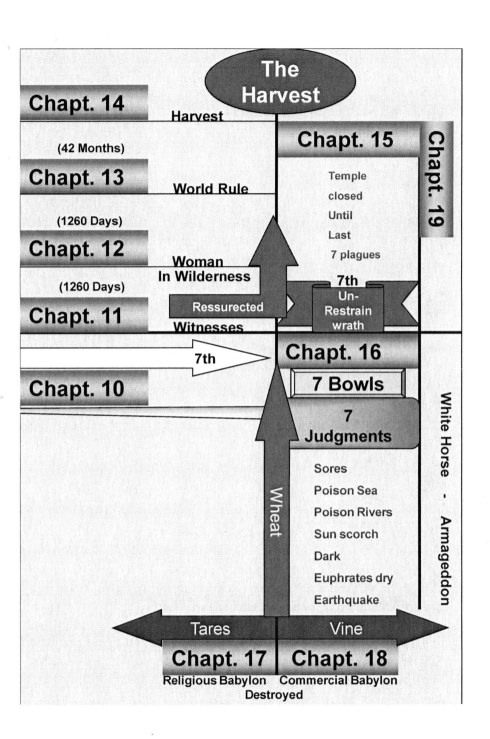